The Spy Web

The
Spy Web

by

FRANCIS NOEL-BAKER

With an Introduction

by

HERBERT A. PHILBRICK

NEW YORK

THE VANGUARD PRESS

CONTENTS

★

Introduction

BY HERBERT A. PHILBRICK

★

On November 25, 1945, a Top Secret document prepared by American security officers was delivered to a
few carefully selected heads of key government departments. One paragraph of the fifty-one page report dealt
with a startling statement made by Igor Gouzenko,
former code clerk in the office of Col. Nicolai Zabotin,
Soviet military attaché in Ottawa, Canada. Gouzenko
had revealed to the FBI—as well as to Canadian authorities—that a number of Soviet espionage agents had penetrated the security defenses of the United States as well
as of the Canadian government.

So successful was this spy web, Gouzenko said, that
in the spring of 1945 one agent of the Soviet Union had
moved into the highest echelons of the United States
Government—as an assistant to the Secretary of State,
Edward R. Stettinius.

Ignacy Samuel Witczak, a modest, retiring instructor
at the University of Southern California, lived quietly
with his wife and two-year-old son, Dickie, on Gramercy
Drive in Los Angeles. He had been a *cum laude* student
at that same University and held a high scholastic
honor, a gold Phi Beta Kappa key. Occasionally he jour-
neyed to Washington "to study the archives of Con-

gress." He spoke Chinese and Japanese fluently. Other than these characteristics, there seemed to be nothing particularly unusual about Ignacy Witczak.

In the late fall of 1945, however, Witczak mysteriously disappeared. A few weeks later, friends of his wife and son saw the pair board a streetcar near Long Beach. They were never seen again.

The answer to these strange events lay in dust-covered records in the basement of a church in Ottawa, Canada. An investigation of old passport files stored there revealed that certain records had been "gimmicked"—tampered with by experts. The real Ignacy Samuel Witczak was a hard-working farmer in Canada. For seven years the man in California, with an alias, a false passport, and using the University as a respectable "cover," had successfully operated as a Soviet espionage agent and a member of the spy web.

In the spring of 1945, an application was placed before Major General Leslie R. Groves, in charge of all security of the "Manhattan Project" (the code name for the secret atomic power-and-weapons development). The application was filed by the National Research Council of Canada, proposing that a prominent British physicist be allowed to visit the United States for one month.

Although the scientist had been "cleared" by British Intelligence, General Groves refused to grant the request.

His vigilance proved not quite enough, however. Only a few months later, on August 9, 1945, a coded message was flashed from a Soviet espionage agent in Canada named "Grant" to the headquarters of Military Intelligence in Moscow. The message stated that "Alek" had stolen extremely important information concerning the

American Atomic Energy Program, including the location of atomic bomb tests in the United States; the type of atomic energy used in the bomb dropped on Japan; secret facts of atomic production; and actual samples of Uranium 233. A short time thereafter, additional material supplied by "Alek," this time including a glass tube with a sample of U.235, was flown by special courier direct to Moscow.

So damaging was the information to the security of this continent that the Prime Minister of Canada immediately cancelled his personal and state appointments and made a hurried, confidential trip to confer with the heads of the American and British governments.

Six months later, Scotland Yard arrested "Alek"—cover name for Dr. Allan Nunn May, the British scientist who had been barred by General Groves.

We would be justified in being distressed even if these shocking facts were isolated indications of treasonous and treacherous activity. Mr. Francis Noel-Baker shows that these are *not* isolated cases, but that they are actually part of the much bigger story of an international spy web, operating under the command of one world headquarters, directed toward a single goal. This web constitutes a danger unparalleled in modern history.

Wisely, Mr. Noel-Baker has restricted his account of five Soviet espionage rings to those facts that reveal the essential patterns common to all of them. Although none of the centers of these five cases was located in the United States, the record shows that the spy web is no respecter of either persons or nations, and that the boundaries of governments mean little more than minor inconveniences to the Red apparatus. For example, in order to send one individual agent of the Canadian group into the United States, the communists had the ready services of Sam Carr, an expert in techniques of illegal crossings, plus a sum of $3,000—the merest trifle to the fourteen men of the Kremlin, in whose hands is concentrated the greatest mass of wealth ever controlled by so few.

Several persistent illusions are effectively demolished by Mr. Noel-Baker's revelations. One is that the Soviet Union was an "ally" of the United States and the free nations during World War II. The record of Soviet espionage activities clearly shows that although there were certain overlapping interests of the various powers directed toward the destruction of Nazi Germany, the Reds at no time ceased their continuing warfare against our own and other non-communist nations.

Another illusion, oft repeated by well-meaning idiots, is that the communist criminal conspiracy is a "political party" composed of "reputable citizens" whose only fault is that they are "non-conformists" who believe in "dissent" and "social reforms."

All communist movements are primarily underground and illegal organizations. That part of the apparatus revealed in the "above ground" movement is a false front—a mask of deception—designed to mislead the unsuspecting victims and to lull them to passive slumber.

For the maintenance of this smoke-screen, the communists employ another agent, as fully dangerous and as much a part of the Soviet espionage apparatus as the spies, although he steals no secrets and handles no microfilm. He is the propaganda expert—the member of the "agit-prop" (agitation and propaganda) division of the party, whose only job is to maintain a tissue of lies designed to present the communist movement in a favorable and acceptable light.

Thus we find that there are two types of spies and agents: first, the hard-core predatory Red who harbors no illusions, and who knows exactly what he is doing and the nature of the cause he serves; and secondly, the "non-party bolshevik," the theoretical Marxist, the fellow traveler who justifies his treason not on the basis of hard reality but on what he is led to believe the Communist Party to be. It is of dubious credit to the MVD (NKVD) that they have been able scientifically to confuse some individuals to the extent that the latter cannot distinguish what is true from false and are persuaded to betray their own homelands and at the same time feel they are doing the "right" thing.

The nature and meaning of the "communist front" takes on a startling new significance in the light of these facts.

Furthermore, this is a story that has not yet reached a conclusion, for the final chapter of the spy web will be written only when the Soviet Union has been destroyed as an imperialist power.

It is a well-known axiom that it is impossible successfully to combat your enemy unless you know your enemy. Francis Noel-Baker has, through his painstaking research and carefully documented exposition of facts, performed a great service by helping us know more about the nature of the enemy confronting the free people and free nations today.

Herbert A. Philbrick

The Spy Web

The Pattern

★

Captain Ormond Leyton Uren was a young officer in a Scottish regiment working on the Army General Staff in London. We met in the summer of 1942. I never knew him well, but I remember talking with him, perhaps three or four times over a glass of beer and a sandwich. He was the kind of casual acquaintance one makes in wartime. He told me that he had joined up two months after war broke out, was commissioned in May 1940, and had served for two years with an infantry unit. I recall him now as a pleasant, ordinary, slightly dull young man with a cheerful smile. For some reason, I see him in flannels, waving a tennis racket—but that is probably just my imagination. At all events, I left for the Middle East soon afterwards and forgot all about him.

I next heard his name about a year later. I was told that he had been cashiered and sentenced to seven years' hard labor as a Russian spy. I was astounded. It seemed so utterly unlikely. But it was true.

In a way, young Uren's story led to the writing of this book. I was curious to solve the mystery of what he had done and why. And that took me on to other similar stories. His own case still cannot be described in detail. But the outline is clear enough: and it fits perfectly into the general pattern of this book.

Uren was a secret communist—though whether he was

actually a party member is not clear. Probably he had been attracted to communism as a student. One day, while he was working on the Staff in London, he told a friend how much he regretted that being a British army officer prevented him from helping the Communist Party or from doing anything practical to show his sympathy with its aims. In the spring of 1943, the friend introduced him to Douglas Frank Springhall, the National Organizer of the Communist Party in Britain and a leading member of its Central Committee. They had several preliminary meetings during one of which Springhall asked Uren for a complete, written report on his life. Uren gave him the report. This was evidently satisfactory, for Springhall began to question Uren about his work on the Staff. Uren then prepared for him a typewritten document describing the whole layout of the military establishment in which he worked and giving other highly secret information. This Springhall was to pass to agents of the Soviet Government in London. A further meeting between Uren and Springhall was arranged for June 17th, but on that morning they were both arrested. At his court martial in October, Uren gave a very typical explanation: "I disclosed the information to Springhall," he said, "to show that I had complete faith in him and that he could have complete trust in me as a sincere believer in communism."

Springhall had meanwhile gone to jail for seven years' hard labor on a charge arising from another case of spying: "Worming vital secrets for the protection of our own fighting men from a Government Department by means of a little woman clerk" was how the judge described it, and added that it was a "detestable offence." The clerk was an Air Ministry official. Springhall had asked her for information for the Russians about the experimental development of secret equipment. She made a frank confession and was sentenced to three months. Springhall himself refused to go into the witness-box or to give any reason for his actions. A big, thick-set, bald-headed man, he was a lifelong communist, had been trained in Russia, and had visited the Far Eastern Red Army. He had previous experience as a defendant, and had already been to prison twice. Throughout the proceedings he sat, silent and surly in the dock, chewing gum. When he was sentenced, the Communist Party announced that it had expelled him and had sacked his wife from the London *Daily Worker* where she was employed. But after his release, he returned to Russia and was reported to have died in Communist China in 1953.

★   ★   ★

The Springhall cases were the first of a long series. At the time they attracted scant attention in the West; Britain was too busy fighting the war—with Soviet Russia as her ally. The first big shock to Western public opinion came when the Canadian case broke after the war had ended. Since then, hardly a month passes without new evidence of communist espionage in one or another country outside the Iron Curtain. Even as this book was being written, revelations from Australia, Germany, Iran, and France added new evidence to a now familiar tale.

Most dramatic of the recent cases is the story of Vladimir Petrov, chief of the N.K.V.D. section of the Soviet Embassy at Canberra, and his wife and assistant, Evdokiya, who both defected and asked the Australian Government for asylum in February 1954. By then, Petrov had served the N.K.V.D. for twenty-four years, had risen to the rank of Colonel and had been decorated with the orders of the Red Banner and the Red Star. His work had taken him abroad before, to China and to Sweden, and he may well have been the oldest surviving officer in the N.K.V.D. on foreign duty. His wife also had a long record of service to the N.K.V.D.—and a grim one. Two of her chiefs were shot in Stalin's great purges of the 1930's. In 1937, her first husband, also an N.K.V.D. man, was sent to forced labor on Solovetsky Island in the White Sea, and her brother met a similar fate a few years later.

Petrov had been in Canberra since February 1951. His official post was Third Secretary and Consul. His real duties were to build up and control a network of Australian communist spies, to smuggle in secret agents for the Soviet Union and to supervise and spy on his colleagues at the Embassy. His wife worked in his office.

Why did these two, apparently devoted Soviet officials, suddenly decide to quit? The answer is simple. For some months, Petrov had been receiving messages from Moscow complaining that he was slack and inefficient in his work. He and his wife well knew the possible consequences of such complaints. Then orders came for his recall.

But there was a still more compelling reason to be afraid. The Petrovs had been appointed to their Canberra posts when Lavrenti Beria was head of the N.K.V.D. Since Beria's disgrace and death, no one with that background could feel safe. And a cipher clerk in the Embassy had told Petrov that the Ambassador, Nicolai Generalov, had been sending secret reports to Moscow that Petrov was intriguing with a pro-Beria clique among the Embassy staff. "I have no wish to return to the Soviet Union," Petrov frankly told Australian officials, "I know that if I did I would be killed." He finally defected three weeks before the date set for his return to Russia.

Self-preservation, in fact, was Petrov's chief motive. It was his wife's motive also; although, when he first left the Embassy, she had decided to return to Moscow where she, unlike him, had relatives. But when Petrov's successor at Canberra, Kouvalenkov, tactlessly told her she was destined for "camps or possibly execution," she too decided to save her life. After a dramatic scene at Darwin airport, she was rescued from the armed Soviet couriers who were escorting her home. But she later explained: "Had I received human treatment from my own people, I would not have hesitated to return to the Soviet Union in spite of my husband's decision."

So it seems that there was nothing very heroic about the Petrovs' defection. And, before taking a final step, Petrov himself was very careful to secure his future. A series of secret meetings with a high Australian security chief preceded his disappearance from the Soviet Embassy. He was promised asylum and protection and a free pardon for all crimes against Australian law committed while he was in Russian service. He was also promised 5,000 Australian pounds (about $11,150), which were paid to him the day after his defection.

Nor did Petrov personally impress the observers who later watched him. One reported that his "tubby figure and pallid moon-face, accentuated by heavy horn-rimmed spectacles, suggested an unsuccessful suburban businessman" and added that "when he emerged from the shadows to tell his story he shattered many popular illusions." Another described him as "a hack official, to whom minor promotions came automatically in a country overloaded with bureaucracy . . . the phlegmatic son of Siberian peasants shuffling through the corridors of oriental subterfuge."

But whatever the Petrovs' motives, or their personal impact on observers, the Australian Government treated their story very seriously indeed. It has revealed the existence of a communist espionage network with wide ramifications in Australia, controlled from the Soviet Embassy. Some of the Russians' local henchmen were so-called "new Australians," recent emigrants from Russia and other Iron Curtain countries. Those who had relatives at home could sometimes, Petrov explained, be blackmailed into helping; others might be bribed by promises of future favors. But his chief source of recruits lay among supporters of the Communist Party of Australia. That Party then claimed 12,000 members. To these must be added some hundreds of secret supporters and fellow travellers, the "cryptos" whom the Party used to bore into trade unions, undermine political groups, and run "friendship societies," "peace committees," and other bogus front organizations. As a political force, the Australian Communist Party was relatively unimportant but, like its fraternal parties in other countries outside the Iron Curtain, it was a useful source of Russian agents. Petrov's leading contacts were communist, and communism provided the motive that made them spy.

Precisely the same motive was apparent in the local men who were to have helped Captain Nicolai Khokhlov of the N.K.V.D. in a dramatically planned assassination of a leading Russian emigré, Georgi Okolovich, at Frankfurt in February 1954. But Khokhlov confided his plans to his intended victim and defected to American security men. His story broke a few days after Petrov's.

The next big spy case to catch the world's attention was revealed by Brigadier General Teymour Bakhtiar, Military Governor of Teheran in August 1954. He announced the uncovering of an extensive spy network in the Iranian armed forces and police. Part of its job was to steal secrets of American military aid to Iran and "specimens" of American arms and equipment. Its leaders were in the closest touch with the illegal Iranian Communist Tudeh Party, and it was controlled from the big Soviet intelligence headquarters at Baku, 200 miles across the northwestern Iranian border. Some 500 suspects were arrested, including twenty Colonels, six heads of Iranian security departments, a second-cousin of the Shah, a Captain of the Imperial Guard, a bodyguard of the Prime Minister's personal staff, and a brother of General Bakhtiar himself. The first ten convicted spies were shot at dawn at a Teheran military barracks on October 19th after pleading guilty. They remained defiant to the end. Further executions followed.

Even before the Iranian case had ended, news came from Paris of major espionage by the French Communist Party involving high police and security officers and the leakage of high state secrets. So efficient was the Paris network that full reports of vital military discussions in the National Defense Council reached communist headquarters the same day. The revelations rocked the French Government and security measures were immediately and drastically tightened.

      ★   ★   ★

So, month by month, the evidence accumulates, evidence that helps to complete our knowledge of a subject by now only too familiar to the experts whose job it is to study and to fight espionage by communists for Soviet Russia. From that evidence, five big cases have been selected for detailed examination in this book. The selection was made for four main reasons. First, because in each case all the significant facts are known, have been checked, and can be published. Second, because together the cases cover a considerable period of time

—roughly from 1933 to 1953—but are all reasonably recent. Third, because they happened in four widely separated countries and under very different conditions; each case had its own special circumstances, but no one can claim—for whatever reason—that the same set of special circumstances applied in each. Finally because, set beside one another, the five cases build up a very complete general picture. If more cases had been included, the repetition of similar situations and events would have added little of value to that picture.

The five cases show that spying by communists for Russia follows a definite and universal pattern into which each separate case fits closely. They also reveal, very clearly, the main ideas, methods, and motives of the people concerned.

In using spies, the aims of the Russian Government are similar to those of other countries, except that it regards every non-communist nation not merely as a potential, but as an actual enemy. It also has a deeper distrust than other governments of all public and open sources of information, and tends to assume that other governments go to the same lengths as it does itself to hide information and mislead foreigners. It therefore attaches a greater significance to the work of spies.

The administrative arrangements inside Russia for organizing and controlling spies abroad are not directly relevant to this book. But the efficiency of the system is certainly affected by the fact that there are several independent and competing intelligence organizations between whom relations are sometimes bad—though that difficulty is not peculiar to Russia. In the following chapters, three intelligence organizations are mentioned. First, there is the so-called security service, which has existed under various names since the revolution: Chela, Ogpu, N.K.V.D., and now—since the amalgamation of the Ministries of State Security and Interior, under the late Lavranti Beria—M.V.D. During most of the period covered by this book its official name was N.K.V.D. and that name has, for convenience, been used throughout. Inside Russia, the hated N.K.V.D. has been responsible for suppressing opposition to the Soviet regime—the "fight against bourgeois, reactionary and counter-revolutionary elements"—and it supervises similar work in Russia's satellites. Outside the Iron Curtain, it operates a complete espionage network, with its own groups of foreign spies; and it is also responsible for supervising and reporting on the opinions and behavior of Soviet officials serving abroad.

Next, there is the military intelligence service, known as the Fourth Bureau of the Red Army, which had offices at 19, Znamensky Street in Moscow. In Soviet Embassies and Legations, its work is normally directed by the Military Attaché, with a staff of Red Army, Red Air Force, or Red Navy officers, though some of them often work under cover as civilian diplomats in other departments, or even as Embassy servants. Soviet military intelligence resembles similar services operated by other Governments, except that its scope seems to be a good deal wider. In Canada during the war, for example, the Soviet Military Attaché also sometimes concerned himself with purely political matters, which seems to have been one of the reasons why he was often at loggerheads with his colleagues of the N.K.V.D., "those uneducated hooligans," as he is reported to have called them.

The third main Soviet secret service is the Comintern —the "Third (Communist) International," which is mainly concerned with political intelligence and with supervising the activities of foreign Communist Parties, but which also, like the other two secret services, operates espionage networks in countries outside the Iron

Curtain. Officially, the Comintern was dissolved in 1943. Actually, it moved its offices back to Textilchikov Street in Moscow, from its wartime headquarters at Ufa, near the Ural mountains, only a few months after its official dissolution. It is at these offices that the personal files of many of Russia's foreign communist spies are kept. Many references to the continuing work of the Comintern have been found in Soviet documents that have lately come into the hands of other Governments.

The limits of the responsibilities of these three Soviet secret services—N.K.V.D., Fourth Bureau, and Comintern—do not seem to be clearly defined, nor do the limits of what information should and what should not interest the Soviet espionage system as a whole. We even know of several cases where Soviet spies spent laborious weeks collecting, in the most devious ways, information that any competent diplomat could easily have obtained through official channels, or even from the local press.

Rivalry between the three secret services, and the fact that their activities often overlap, has been a major weakness of the whole Soviet spy system. Sometimes, they even find themselves competing for the use of the same foreign spy; their methods of recruiting and organizing their spies are very similar.

In almost all the big Russian spy rings that have been exposed since 1944, the spies were taking direct orders from Soviet officials. But these officials rarely did any actual spying themselves. Their active spies were never Russians and were usually citizens of the country in which they operated.

There is no recorded case where a Soviet Russian has worked successfully as a secret agent in a foreign country and it is not difficult to find the reason. Soviet officials are conspicuous and naturally liable to be suspected; and, apart from them, there are no Soviet citizens living abroad. Further, not many members of the Soviet bureaucracy—a clumsy, cumbersome machine—have the finesse and quickness needed by a spy. Finally, an efficient spy must have an intimate knowledge of the foreign country in which he is working and of the day-to-day habits of its people. But Soviet citizens have been isolated from the outside world and denied such knowledge for more than a generation.

Other Governments seeking to run efficient espionage services might find these difficulties insuperable. But the Soviet Government has one great asset—the Communist Parties throughout the free world. As spies it almost always uses locally recruited communists, and the initial recruiting is done for it by the local Communist Party.

Most of the exceptions have been when someone was wanted with a special qualification that no available communist happened to possess. In Japan, for example, the spy ring described later in this book needed a qualified translator with technical knowledge. In Canada, the Soviet Military Attaché wanted an expert for helping to forge passports. Local communists could not be found to do these jobs. In such cases, ordinary professional agents were employed but this happens very rarely.

There is one other category of people—apart from the communists—whom the Russians systematically seek to use wherever they can find them: emigrants and refugees from Russia and the satellite states who have left relatives behind them. In such cases, the inducement offered by the Russians is threat of reprisals against the relatives or, sometimes, promises to allow the relatives to escape from behind the Iron Curtain. But there is no known case where such a promise actually has been kept.

Nevertheless, the bulk of Russia's spies, in all the networks of which we know, came from the local Communist Parties. It follows that the chief motive—and usually the only important motive—of almost every spy who works for the Russians is ideological. The Communist Party supplies the necessary ideas. It does this so effectively that any really loyal party member or supporter is always eager and ready to spy for Russia, if given the opportunity.

Of course, if you were to ask a militant American, Canadian, or Australian communist if he and his comrades were all potential spies for Russia, he would indignantly deny it; that is, unless he knew that you, too, were a Communist Party member yourself—in which case you would not ask the question. But, in fact, that is exactly what any really well indoctrinated communist must be. He is expected to give absolute loyalty to the Soviet Union, at the expense of any other loyalty whatsoever.

Leading communists in all countries have explained and justified this need for overriding loyalty to Russia. Perhaps the clearest explanation of the reasoning involved was given by a prominent former British communist, Douglas Hyde. Hyde said: "Communism is necessary and desirable above all else. The fight for communism stretches across the world, which is divided horizontally by the two opposing classes and not vertically by different races and nations. . . . But at one point in that world front there is a whole nation on my side, a great State, the U.S.S.R., where a strong point has been established, around which all future battles will tend to turn and without which any other local victories must fail. At all cost, therefore, Russia, bastion of communism, must be defended. The defeat of the U.S.S.R. would mean the end of any chance of world communism for generations.

"Therefore, in order to get my communist Britain, I

must at all costs work to assist the continued survival of the Socialist Sixth of the world. Who attacks Russia attacks my hope of a communist Britain. In helping Russia with all the means at his disposal and at any price, therefore, the British communist is working for a better Britain, the French communist for a better France, the Icelandic communist for a better Iceland. He is, in his own eyes and that of his Party, the super-patriot. The need is for Russia at all costs to survive, and anything, anything at all, which contributes to this is possible."

This need for communists to give absolute loyalty to Russia, at the expense of every other loyalty whatever, is emphasized again and again in Communist Party propaganda. It has, in fact, been officially accepted as the one supreme test of the political understanding of a party member or supporter. It explains why the spies in this book, and others like them, were quite unaffected by ordinary sentiments of national patriotism, family affection or personal interest—and why they had few qualms about becoming Russian spies.

In many countries—particularly in relatively prosperous and socially stable countries like the United States, Britain, or Sweden, for example—the secret and illegal activities of the Communist Party are often much more important than their open work. In those countries, communists are negligible as a purely political force. Their only real importance is as an active or potential fifth column. Their local leaders realize this and so, of course, do the Russians.

★   ★   ★

What those Russians who are concerned with spying think of the motives and ideas of their spies, the five cases that follow do not make clear. They seem a little cynical at times; and that is perhaps only natural for

busy officials for whom spying is, after all, simply a routine for producing practical results. At all events they
take the cautious view that ideology, useful though it is,
is not enough. Therefore, however fervent and idealistic
a spy may be, there always comes a time when the Russians give him money. They calculate perhaps that ideas
are often unstable things. One cannot be certain that the
ideas of a man—even the most militant communist—may
not change. And then, if they are his only motive, he
becomes unreliable as a spy. But from the Russians'
point of view it is essential that the spy shall continue
to take orders under any circumstances, even if those
orders are only to stop spying and not talk. The giving
of money, in fact, makes it possible to use blackmail
against a spy, should that become necessary in the future. Other forms of blackmail are also used, but money
is often the most convenient. There is also the advantage,
for the Russians, that the acceptance of money not only
makes a spy feel more irrevocably committed to his spying—it is a concrete symbol of his servitude—but it may
also degrade him in his own eyes, and a man who has
consciously degraded himself is less likely to summon up
courage to disobey.

So the Russians have developed the habit of insisting
that all their spies should take money—and sign receipts
for it—whether they want it or not and even when they
are shocked and revolted (as they sometimes are) by
the suggestion. I have been told by people who knew
them, that it is inconceivable that some of the spies in
this book—Dr. Nunn May for example—could have accepted Russian bribes. But they did, and have admitted
that they did. Some of them considered the matter an
unimportant detail, other perhaps accepted it as part
of the discipline to which they had surrendered.

★   ★   ★

The usual technique for recruiting a communist into Russian service is quite simple. For a time, he is watched unobtrusively by one of his party comrades. Then that comrade (or another) sounds him out, cautiously and in general terms. If he seems suitable, a complete dossier of his past life is prepared, often by the recruit himself. This, together with a photograph, is handed to a Russian who sends it, with his own observations, back to Moscow. In due course, the Russian organization concerned signifies its approval. The spy is now usually warned to dissociate himself from the Communist Party—unless he has already done so—and to have no further contact with its members. He is then given a code name and put to work. He may either be in direct contact with a Russian whom he meets secretly from time to time, or he may pass his reports through one or more local contact-men or by wireless. At all events, the spy should not normally know the real identity of his Russian master, nor for which particular Russian organization he is working.

It so happens that the Russians rarely use women spies. Perhaps the reasons are those given by one of their most successful spies, Richard Sorge. "Women are absolutely unfit for espionage work. They have no understanding of political and other affairs and I have never received satisfactory information from them. . . . Even upper-class women have no comprehension of what has been said by their husbands and are, therefore, very poor sources of information . . . in my opinion, no woman in the world has the aptitude for espionage work. . . . In the last analysis espionage operations must be performed by a man with a good education and a clear mind." It may have been coincidence that one of Sorge's own women spies was responsible for the destruction of his spy ring, and that another woman was, very indirectly, responsible for the breakdown of one of the rings in Sweden.

The information which the spies collect, varies, of course, according to the period and country in which they work. In the five cases that follow, all the spies were concerned largely—and most of them exclusively—with military secrets. They all knew (even the Greeks whose contact with Russia was indirect) that the chief use—and often the only possible one—to which their information could be put was to help Russian preparations for a war against the country in which they spied.

★   ★   ★

Not all the general statements in this chapter apply to every spy in the five cases. Sorge, for example, though he worked in Japan and cooperated with Japanese communists, was a German recruited through the German Communist Party. Likewise, so far as is known, there were no Russians in Athens supervising the Vavoudes ring: the supervision was indirect, through the exiled Greek communist leaders in Bucharest. And in Sweden Enbom and nearly all his fellow spies remained in close touch with the Swedish Communist Party. There are other exceptions to the general rules: but the chief interest of those exceptions is to show how very closely the various cases fit the general pattern.

The Case
of Doctor Sorge

Doctor Richard Sorge was probably the most successful individual spy who has ever worked for Soviet Russia. He came to Tokyo in September 1933 and had practically completed his assignment there when he was arrested in October 1941. During those eight years, no foreign country was of greater importance to the Russians than Japan. As the Mikado's armies overran Manchuria and then turned against the rest of China, Soviet defense plans and foreign policy began to depend more and more on Japan's intentions and military strength. When the second world war broke out, the need for reliable intelligence from Tokyo became still more urgent. Would the Japanese strike north against the Asiatic frontiers of the Soviet Union, or would they turn south against British and American possessions in the Pacific? After Hitler's attack on Russia in June 1941, Soviet military survival depended on the answer to that question.

During all this time, Richard Sorge was sending to Moscow a steady flow of vitally important secret information, stolen from the highest official sources, which enabled the Russians to predict with great accuracy each new military and diplomatic move by the Japanese Government. It has even been claimed that the successful defense of Moscow against the Nazi armies was largely due to Dr. Sorge, that it was his reports which convinced the Russian generals that they could safely move large numbers of troops away from the Eastern border as reinforcements for the Western front. Without those reinforcements Moscow would certainly have fallen.

The story of Sorge's spy ring is mainly the story of Sorge himself: a bold and clever man who early in his life became a communist fanatic. "Had I lived under peaceful social conditions and in a peaceful environment of political development," he wrote later, "I should perhaps have been a scholar—certainly not an espionage agent." But the conditions in which he grew up in Germany, during and after the first world war, were far from peaceful. Like many others of his generation, he was led by his experiences of that time into the Communist Party, which he served, in the most dangerous of all ways, for the rest of his life.

It was partly chance which sent Sorge, a German communist with a Russian mother, to spy in Japan. (Towards the end of his assignment in Japan, he was trying to be sent back to his native Germany to continue his spy work there.) Two of his chief assistants were Europeans, like himself. But the rest were all Japanese, and all but one were recruited from Japanese communist organizations. It was a tribute to their communist fervor that they were ready to spy against their own Asiatic country for a predominantly European nation in a war against Europeans.

War and preparation for war are the background to the Sorge case. Much of the information which he sent to Moscow would have been of great value to the Western Powers. But even after Russia was invaded and herself became an ally of the West, none of his information was ever passed on.

Since the war, the Russian Government has been more secretive about the case of Richard Sorge than about any of the other known cases of Russian spies. One can only guess the reasons.

II

The Nazi Correspondent

★

Richard Sorge was born in 1895, at Baku in South Russia, where his father was working as an engineer in a German oil company. His mother was a Russian. A few years later the family moved back to Berlin, and there Richard spent his childhood in the comfortable atmosphere of a prosperous middle-class home. His father was a typical, patriotic German nationalist, very much aware of his money and his social status. But Richard was already rather different from the other small boys of his own age and class. "I was a bad pupil, defied school regulations, was obstinate and wilful and rarely opened my mouth," he later wrote. But at history, literature and philosophy he was soon well ahead of his form-mates, and his eager interest in politics earned him the nickname of "Prime Minister."

He was eighteen and a half when the first world war broke out and had just been spending his summer holiday in Sweden. Without telling his family, he at once volunteered for the German army and enlisted as a private. After only six weeks of basic training on a Berlin parade ground, he and his comrades were sent straight to the Western front where a great battle was raging on the banks of the Yser river. Early in 1915 he was wounded, was sent home to convalesce and was discharged. Before he was completely well, he volunteered

21

once more and this time was sent to the Eastern front. A year later he was again wounded and sent home, and again volunteered for front-line service. By now conditions in Germany were growing very bad, and in the army Sorge came into contact with disillusioned soldiers who were already talking revolution. Early in 1917 he was wounded for a third time and was seriously ill for several months. When he recovered, he went back to his studies at the University of Berlin and decided to abandon medicine for economics and political science.

It was now the summer of 1917 and the German economy had begun to crumble. Sorge's own family, like many others of the German middle class, had lost its money. He began to think of himself as a member of the proletariat, and started to make a detailed study of Marxist writings. Then came the Russian revolution which seemed to Sorge to answer all the problems of the collapsing pre-war social system. "I decided not only to support the movement theoretically and ideologically," he wrote years later, "but to become an actual part of it. All the solutions to my personal and material problems at which I have arrived since then have perforce stemmed from that decision."

From Berlin, Sorge went to the University at Kiel and then on to Hamburg. At Kiel he joined his first revolutionary political organization and in 1918 took a small part in the mutiny of the German sailors at the naval base there. Next year at Hamburg he formally became a communist when the students' group of which he was the secretary was absorbed by the newly established German Communist Party.

In 1920, Sorge took his Doctorate in political science at Hamburg and then found a job as a schoolteacher at Aachen in the West German coal-fields. By now, he was an active Communist Party worker, and was sent for by the Central Committee in Berlin to report on conditions in his area and to receive new instructions. At Aachen, his chief tasks were the training of party members and propaganda among the miners. Once during school holidays, he ran a local communist newspaper for two months while its editor was in jail. At the end of 1922, he was discharged by his school for his political activities, and became a coal-miner. The work was hard and he was hampered by his war wounds; but he welcomed the experience and his propaganda among his fellow workers was most successful. As he moved from pit to pit, he left behind him a series of new Communist Party groups. When he tried to extend his recruiting activities to Holland, however, by taking work in the neighboring coalfields across the frontier, he was dismissed from a Dutch mine and deported back to Germany. By now he was notorious in the Aachen coal mines, too. The managements all refused him work and the German authorities threatened to turn him over to the Allies who had occupied the Rhineland. He went back to Berlin to discuss future plans with the Central Committee of his party.

He was first offered a paid job with the party's central propaganda department, which he refused. Finally, it was agreed that he should take a post at the University of Frankfurt, while at the same time acting as a contact man between the local party there and headquarters in Berlin, handling party funds and helping to direct propaganda. This was his first experience of secret undercover work. When an armed revolt broke out in Saxony and, for a short time, set up a "workers' republic" there, Sorge was sent on frequent special missions to take instructions to the insurgents' leaders.

It was in 1924 that he was given the assignment which was to change his life. That year a communist convention was held at Frankfurt. Sorge was a delegate. But in addition he had the important task of guarding four leading members of the Comintern who had come secretly and illegally from Moscow to attend the convention: Pyatnitsky, Manuilsky, Kuusinen and Lozovsky. Thirty years later, three of these men were still prominent Soviet leaders: Kuusinen was a deputy chairman of the Supreme Soviet, Manuilsky, Foreign Minister of the Ukraine, and Lozovsky a deputy Foreign Minister of the Soviet Union.

By the end of the convention at Frankfurt, Sorge was on close and friendly terms was the four delegates from Moscow. They invited the tough, enthusiastic young German to come to Russia to work for them in the Comintern. His local party leaders in Berlin agreed and he arrived in Moscow in January 1925. His name was taken from the lists of German party members and he joined the Communist Party of the Soviet Union.

For the next four years he worked for the intelligence division of the Comintern, preparing reports on the activities of foreign communist parties and on political and economic conditions in their countries. He dealt mainly with Northwestern Europe and used both published material and secret information from party sources. It was on the basis of reports like his that the leaders of the Comintern decided their instructions to foreign parties. Twice during this period Sorge was sent abroad himself: to Scandinavia in 1927, and to Scandinavia and Britain in 1928. His tasks were to study the problems of the local parties, discuss them with their leaders and report back to Moscow. At the same time, he was expected to prepare more general intelligence reports about conditions in the countries which he visited.

Of this system of combining party organization work with espionage he strongly disapproved. A spy, he felt, should not involve himself in the internal quarrels of local communists (of which he had seen a good deal at that time, particularly in Norway, where the party was going through a major crisis). Besides, to work effectively a spy must work in secret, and contact with known communists was bound, sooner or later, to compromise him with the police. He reported these views to his chiefs when he returned to Moscow from England early in 1929.

Until that year, spying had been only a small, almost an incidental, part of Sorge's work: no more than comes the way of many Communist Party members. In Moscow, his job in the Comintern office really amounted to political research. On his journeys, he had been mostly concerned with party organization. Admittedly, he had travelled under cover as a special correspondent of a German magazine, and he did not advertise the real reason for his journeys. But it is doubtful whether, had he been exposed or even arrested at this time, he would have run any very serious risk. A deportation order was probably the worst he had to fear. But his next assignment was entirely different. He now started far more important and far more dangerous work.

On his arrival in Moscow from Britain, Sorge had a long discussion with Pyatnitsky, one of his chiefs in the Comintern who was also one of the four men who had originally invited him to Russia. As a result of this discussion, Pyatnitsky saw General Beldin, the chief of Military Intelligence, who happened to be Pyatnitsky's close personal friend. They agreed that Sorge should be transferred to Beldin's organization.

At this time, Military Intelligence was already the most important of the various espionage services which worked from Moscow. The Comintern was, of course, mainly concerned with organizing and directing com-

munist parties abroad. The foreign spy-rings run by the
secret police were chiefly interested in counter-espionage
and watching anti-Soviet organizations. Military Intelligence, on the other hand, covered a very wide field. It
controlled not only the Soviet Military Attachés serving
abroad but also, sometimes through them and sometimes
directly, its own networks of spies. Its activities were not
confined to straight military espionage, and it collected
secret information on all important subjects. It was well
organized, efficiently administered and very adequately
financed. It had the additional advantage of being in
close contact with high party leaders in Russia, who
came to rely on it more and more as a general source of
secret information.

Sorge himself was already known to Military Intelligence, both through his work for the Comintern and also
because, some years before, when he was still in Germany, he had been in touch with one of its local networks, which had wanted to recruit him as a spy. He was
now asked whether he wished to return to Europe, or
to serve in the Far East. He chose the Far East, and left
for Shanghai towards the end of 1929.

With his transfer from the Comintern to Military Intelligence, Sorge's personal status changed. He ceased
to be the servant of international communism and became a full-time spy for Soviet Russia. But to Sorge himself, this change was unimportant. Like him, many other
devoted foreign communists had started their work in
the Communist Party and had later moved to jobs under
the Russian Government. For them, international communism and Soviet Russia were now one and the same
thing. As Sorge himself wrote later, "the shift in my activities meant a transfer to new work designed to further
Soviet foreign policy and bolster Soviet defenses against
external attack. Such activities are as important and

universal an expression of communist ideals as are Comintern activities on behalf of individual communist parties." And he added: "Through our work, we contribute directly to the welfare of the Soviet Union . . . and indirectly to the cause of world revolution."

As a Soviet spy, Sorge had many personal qualifications: a good mind, steady nerves and a keen organizing ability, combined with complete devotion to the Government of Russia. But he also had one grave disadvantage: he was already known as an active communist. Among his friends in Germany, he had made no secret of his political views nor of the fact that he had worked for the Comintern. He had even published a political pamphlet and two political books; the books had been widely read in Germany and had been translated into Russian. By 1929 he certainly had a considerable dossier with the German police.

How Sorge managed to conceal his past is the biggest mystery of his whole story. He took no obvious steps to do so. He changed neither his appearance nor his name. Instead, he seems to have decided to take a colossal, calculated risk and simply ignore the whole of his early life. It was a fantastic piece of bluff—and it was a complete success.

★   ★   ★

Four years later, a new German newspaper correspondent arrived in Tokyo, a tall, gaunt man with rather hunched shoulders, brown hair, a lined, expressive face and penetrating eyes. His clothes were untidy and he had an air of dissipation. He was a hard drinker and was known to like variety in women, with whom he was unusually successful. In conversation, he was cynical, dogmatic and quick-tempered, and was often extremely offensive to people whose opinions he despised. Some of his colleagues cordially disliked him and among them he had the reputation of being a typically arrogant, swashbuckling Nazi; he was in fact a Nazi Party member. But he was also a very able journalist and, although he had never been to Japan before and had worked for only three years in China, it was not long before he was recognized as something of an expert on Japanese and Far Eastern affairs. Among the four papers which he represented in Tokyo were two leading European dailies: the *Frankfurter Zeitung* and the *Handelsblatt* of Amsterdam.

In Tokyo, Richard Sorge the German newspaperman soon became well known. He found some acquaintances who had already met him during his three years as a correspondent in Shanghai. He quickly made others among members of the local Nazi Party and in the German club. To the staff of the Germany Embassy he brought letters of introduction from German diplomats whom he had known in China. He was soon on good terms with the Japanese officials who dealt with the foreign press. Nothing, in fact, could have been more open or seemed more normal than his behavior. For eight years, he lived a double life in Tokyo and never made a single blunder. The tough, wild-living Nazi journalist perfectly concealed the industrious, calculating Russian spy.

From Military Intelligence in Moscow, Sorge's instructions were comprehensive; he had a wide field to cover. Above all, his masters were interested in the security of Russia's Eastern frontier. This meant that his chief task was to keep them constantly informed on Japan's military plans and to be able to predict, at any time, whether the Japanese armies in Manchuria were preparing to attack Russia. Meanwhile, he had to follow closely the progress of the war in China and Japan's relations with other countries, particularly Germany, with whom she signed the Anti-Comintern Pact in 1936. He was also naturally concerned with the condition and movements of all Japanese armed forces, with the state of Japan's economy, and with political developments. He was not expected simply to pass on isolated scraps of secret information, but to evaluate and analyze each item and then to fit it into a general picture of Japan's strength and intentions. He was encouraged to draw conclusions from the information he reported and even, at times, to make suggestions to the Russian Government. He was, in fact, much more than a simple spy—he was also a kind of secret political adviser.

The difficulties of such an assignment in Tokyo in the 1930's were considerable. The Japanese Government was particularly hostile to Russia and kept the Soviet Embassy under such close police surveillance that effective espionage by Soviet diplomats was practically impossible. That, of course, was one reason for sending to Tokyo a man like Richard Sorge. But the Japanese police did not confine their activities to Russians; they were intensely suspicious of all foreigners and obsessed by the fear of spies. At the same time, Japanese officials and politicians were cautious and secretive, Japanese politics were exceedingly complicated, and the wildest rumors flourished about every important topic. In the circumstances, to establish reliable and safe sources of secret information needed great skill and very careful planning.

Sorge, however, was well prepared for his new task. He had already learned a good deal about the technique of espionage during his three years in Shanghai. Though, for a spy, conditions there, in the relative freedom of an international city, were far easier than in Tokyo, much of his experience was useful. He had become familiar with such matters as the handling of under-cover cour-

iers, secret wireless stations and the recruiting of local
agents. At the same time, he had made an intensive study
of Far Eastern questions. He had learned to speak the
Shanghai dialect of Chinese and he had taken a very
genuine interest in Chinese history and art. Foreseeing
a possible future mission in Japan, he had also done
much reading about that country. He continued his Japanese studies when he got to Tokyo. They were necessary
to him both as a newspaper correspondent and for his
spy work, and he was in no great hurry to start spying.
In fact, for his first three months in Japan, he deliberately
did nothing about his secret assignment. He knew that
the Japanese police would be watching him particularly
closely immediately after his arrival, and in any case
his chiefs in Moscow had repeatedly warned him, for his
own safety, to take his time.

★   ★   ★

Sorge had left Moscow in May 1933. He had gone first
to Berlin. Hitler had just come to power in Germany and
Sorge hastened to join the Nazi Party. How he succeeded
in doing so and why no one turned up his communist
record is still quite unexplained. Possibly secret communists were helping him both in the Nazi Party and in the
Gestapo. At all events he was accepted without question.
He seems to have had no trouble either, in arranging his
accreditation with the *Frankfurter Zeitung* and his other
papers.

With his cover so well settled, Sorge went on to Paris.
There he booked in at a prearranged hotel where, next
day, a member of the French network of the Russian
Military Intelligence gave him the name and address of
a man who had already been sent from Paris to Tokyo
to be Sorge's chief European assistant. He also told him
the secret passwords by which he could identify this

man. Then he gave Sorge his instructions for the next step on his journey. Sorge duly sailed for New York and, on arrival, took a room at the Lincoln Hotel on West Forty-fourth Street. A second contact man came to see him at the hotel and ordered him to go on to Chicago. There, in the grounds of the World's Fair on the shore of Lake Michigan, he met an American journalist. This man was yet another representative of the Russian Military Intelligence. He told Sorge how to find a Japanese assistant who was being sent from the United States to Tokyo to work with him. From Chicago, Sorge travelled to Vancouver and caught a ship for Yokohama. He arrived on September 6th.

After three months in Tokyo, Sorge felt that he was well established as a Nazi newspaper correspondent, and began to organize his spy-ring. The first step was to make contact with his European assistant about whom he had been told in Paris. He found him without difficulty. Like Sorge himself, Branko de Voukelitch had also come to Tokyo posing as a journalist. He was the correspondent of the Yugoslav daily newspaper *Politica*, and of a French weekly magazine. He was tall, thick-set and 29 years old, the son of a Serbian army officer, who had gone to Paris to study law and had there joined the Communist Party in January 1932. He was a talkative young man with a taste for discussing with his foreign colleagues politico-philosophical abstractions which became increasingly more abstract as his inadequate English and hardly more adequate French gave out under the strain of self-expression. His wife Edith, who had come to Tokyo with him, was a Dane: "a dull woman" his colleagues called her, and privately de Voukelitch was beginning to agree. They had been in Tokyo since the previous February.

De Voukelitch had only been a member of the Com-

munist Party in France for a few months before he joined
a spy-ring there. He was recruited by a Baltic woman
who was a Russian agent and whom he knew simply as
Olga. It was *Olga* who had told him of his assignment
in Japan and had arranged for him and his wife to sail
from Marseilles at the end of December 1932. On arrival
in Tokyo, they had first lived in a block of flats and had
then moved into a private house in the residential district of Ushigome. De Voukelitch, who let it be known
he was an enthusiastic amateur photographer, had at
once had a dark room built in the new house.

Some time after his arrival, de Voukelitch had made
contact with a certain *Bernhardt,* a man about whom he
had been told in Paris. *Bernhardt's* real identity has
never been revealed. He was a wireless operator trained
by the Russian Military Intelligence, and almost nothing
else is known about him except that Sorge later complained that he was highly inefficient.

The third member of the ring who was already in
Tokyo waiting for Sorge's arrival was his Japanese assistant who had been sent from the United States. He was
a thirty-year-old artist who was born on the island of
Okinawa but had lived most of his life in California.
After graduating from an American art school in 1925,
he had opened a restaurant in Los Angeles with three
other Japanese. But he spent most of his time painting.
He had married when he was twenty-five. Throughout
his life he was troubled with tuberculosis. His name was
Miyagi Yotoku.

Miyagi had come to America in the year of the Russian
revolution. It was also a time of strong anti-Japanese
feeling in California. He had been shocked, he later said,
"by the inconsistencies of American capitalism, the tyr-
anny of the governing classes, and above all the inhuman
discrimination against the Asiatic races. I came to the

conclusion that communism was the cure for all these ills." The result was that in 1929 he joined two "front" organizations which were affiliated with the American Communist Party, and in 1931, influenced by a fellow Japanese-American named Yano, who had just returned from Moscow, he joined the party itself as a secret member and under a false name. Just a year later, Yano and a European whom Miyagi did not know but who called himself an agent of the Comintern, came to see Miyagi in Los Angeles. They told him that the Party wanted him to go to Tokyo. This was almost exactly the same time that in Paris a similar message was being given to de Voukelitch by the mysterious *Olga*.

But Miyagi hesitated. He was busy with his painting, and he was not particularly enthusiastic about travelling to Tokyo where he had never been before. He managed to delay his journey for a year. Then, one day in September 1933, another Communist Party member whom he knew well, a man named Roy, visited him at his home. He said that he must leave immediately for Japan but that he would not be away for more than three months. He gave Miyagi two hundred dollars for his journey, and told him to watch a Tokyo newspaper for a certain advertisement. He also gave him a special dollar note. He explained that the man who identified himself by showing Miyagi a dollar note with the next consecutive serial number would be his new chief in Japan. Miyagi sailed in October 1933 expecting to be away for a brief visit. He left behind him all his personal possessions and also his young wife. He never saw her or America again.

Three months later Miyagi opened a copy of the *Japan Advertiser* in Tokyo. In the personal column, he saw a collector's note asking for Ukiyo-ye prints and books on Japanese art. There was a box number for replies. In accordance with Roy's instructions, Miyagi sent a prearranged answer. In a few days, he met de Voukelitch at the Ueno art museum. A little later, de Voukelitch introduced him to Richard Sorge. It was Sorge who had the second dollar note.

In this way, the beginnings of the new spy-ring were established. The plans so carefully laid in General Beldin's office had worked without a hitch. Three key men, a German, a Japanese and a Yugoslav, had been moved across the world to Tokyo from Moscow, Los Angeles and Paris. It was a striking demonstration of the scope and efficiency of Russian Military Intelligence. Sorge was now ready to start work.

III

Ambassador's Adviser

★

Moscow is five thousand miles from Tokyo, well beyond the range of the most powerful portable transmitter. But somewhere in Siberia there is a big Russian relay station. Neither Sorge nor his wireless operator knew its exact location; they called it by the code-name *Wiesbaden* and guessed that it was at Vladivostok, Komsomolsk or Khabarovsk. It was to *Wiesbaden* that they sent their messages for Moscow. Each one was first written out by Sorge in English or German—he never used Russian—and then enciphered into groups of numbers. The key was based on the pages of the official German *Statistical Yearbook,* four volumes which looked innocent enough on Sorge's crowded bookshelves. The system used was impossible to break.

Sorge's operator used a small "home-made" set which could be quickly packed away into a big black brief-case. He moved it after each transmission from one to another of four or five wooden houses in Tokyo, leaving no trace behind him except a fairly innocent-looking wireless aerial. In this way he beat the watchful Japanese radio interception experts whose direction finders could only fix a small transmitter to within a radius of two miles. For several years Sorge's secret station was in touch with *Wiesbaden* about once every six days.

The spy-ring's second channel of communication was

35

by courier. Who these Soviet couriers were and how they travelled was their secret. The members of the ring met them only for a few moments at intervals of several months. Usually, until the war began, the meetings took place in Shanghai or Hong Kong. Later, the couriers sometimes came as far as Tokyo. Elaborate recognition signs and passwords were always arranged in advance by wireless.

Once, Sorge himself went to meet a courier in Hong Kong. He waited for him in a crowded restaurant. At a few minutes after three, the stranger entered. Deliberately, he took a long, black Manila cigar from his pocket and held it, unlighted, in his hand. Seeing this signal, Sorge walked up to the counter and took from his own pocket a conspicuous-looking pipe. The courier then lit his cigar and Sorge lit his pipe. The identification was now complete, and the two men left the restaurant separately and walked round to a nearby park. Then, the courier started their brief conversation. "Greetings from Katcha," he said. "Greetings from Gustav," Sorge answered. In a moment two small packages had changed hands and the meeting was over. The two men walked slowly away in opposite directions.

Sometimes colored parcels were used as recognition signals between the courier and his contact-man. Once the courier was instructed to go at a prearranged time to a small eating house in Tokyo, sit at a particular table and order a special Japanese dish. The arrangements were always foolproof and they were devised to look completely innocent if either party happened to be under observation. The "mail" itself usually took the form of little rolls of microfilm carefully wrapped in a small package. The photography was done in de Voukelitch's dark room, and sometimes, over a period of four or five months, there might be twenty-five or thirty films with the photographs of several hundred sheets of paper. In return for these, the courier would hand over money: bundles of American dollars or Japanese banknotes. There might also be papers or microfilm from Moscow, but usually instructions only came by wireless.

★   ★   ★

Once his communications with Moscow were established, Sorge's next task was to recruit more spies. This was the most dangerous part of all his work, for Tokyo was full of informers, provocateurs and secret police. One false move, one careless conversation, might easily bring disaster. For his safety, Sorge had been forbidden to have direct contact with the Japanese Communist Party. Normally, recruiting was always done through contact-men, and Sorge himself never met more than a very few members of his ring. In the end it became a big organization, with nearly twenty regular Japanese spies besides his European assistants. After Sorge himself, by far its most important member was Ozaki Hidemi.

In his own way, Ozaki was almost as remarkable a man as his chief. He was a brilliant young journalist in his early thirties, a man with a big reputation in Tokyo and close connections with the highest political circles. That he was also a convinced communist was a secret known only to Sorge and a very few trusted associates. As a boy he had lived in Formosa, where his father, like him a professional journalist, was editor of a daily paper. There he had developed a strong interest in the Chinese (who formed the majority of the local population) and an intense hatred of Japanese militarism and colonial methods. From school at Formosa, Ozaki went on to Tokyo and took his law degree at the Imperial University in 1925. While a student he began to read all the books he could find on China and also to study the works of Marx, Engels and Lenin. So far as is known, he never became a card-carrying member of the Communist Party.

After a year of post-graduate study, Ozaki joined the staff of the Tokyo *Asahi Shimbun,* was transferred a little later to the Osaka office of the *Asahi,* and was sent as its correspondent to Shanghai in 1928. There his communist views and his interest in China brought him into contact with a well-known American journalist and author, a devoted propagandist of the Chinese Communists named Agnes Smedley. It was through her that he first met Richard Sorge at the end of 1930. For some unexplained reason, Sorge was introduced to him as "Mr. Johnson, the American correspondent." He and Sorge soon became friendly and began to meet at frequent intervals in Shanghai restaurants and at Miss Smedley's home. Sorge found him a very intelligent and reliable informant. After two years in Shanghai he was already a considerable expert on Chinese problems, he knew a great deal about the Chinese Communist Party, and he was naturally also well informed about Japanese policy in China. How much Sorge told him about his spying at that time is not known. But he must have had a shrewd suspicion that Sorge's interest in the subjects they discussed was not purely journalistic.

In 1932, Ozaki returned to Japan and did not see Sorge for four years. When they met again in Tokyo in 1936 (they were casually introduced by a Dutchman who did not know that they already knew each other) Ozaki had become one of the leading Japanese authorities on China and was on intimate terms with members of the personal staff of Prince Konoye. Next year, Konoye became President of the House of Peers. Soon afterwards, Ozaki was appointed a government consultant on Chinese affairs and also joined Konoye's circle of advisers: an extremely influential group of "bright young men" nick-named in Tokyo, because of the time at which they often met, the "Breakfast Club."

Ozaki joined Sorge's Tokyo spy-ring, and became an invaluable helper. He had access to the deepest secrets of the Cabinet and to official documents of all kinds, and was sometimes even in a position to influence government policy himself. When Konoye was out of office between January 1939 and July 1940, he still knew more about behind-the-scenes politics than most men in Tokyo. His reports gave Sorge a better insight into Japanese intentions than he could have got from a hundred less well-placed spies.

During all this time, none of Ozaki's official colleagues had the remotest inkling of his views. That he could be a spy would have seemed to them utterly fantastic. In the five authoritative books he wrote on China he gave no hint of communist sympathies. But though Sorge never told him exactly who his masters were in Moscow, he realized quite clearly the purpose of what he was doing. "I guessed at once," he afterwards said, "that Sorge was a functionary of the International Communist Party engaged in espionage activities. My reason for deciding to cooperate with him was that . . . I believed in communism and had decided to become active as a communist. I felt that I would be doing something of real importance assisting Sorge in espionage work on behalf of the Comintern."

Ozaki's main task was, of course, to supply Sorge with Japanese political information, for which he generally used his own direct sources. But he was also in touch with a few of Sorge's lesser spies, some of whom he himself recruited into the ring. One of the first was Kawai Teikichi, a contemporary of Ozaki whom Ozaki had met when Kawai was a reporter in Shanghai. He had introduced Sorge to him at that time (by the improbable name of "Robinson Crusoe") and Kawai had then started to make written reports for Sorge. When he returned to Japan he joined the spy-ring there. He had an immense personal admiration for Ozaki, and had become a communist while he was in Shanghai. "Since I had already accepted communism," he afterwards said, "and since I supported the Comintern and believed in the desirability of an international communist society, I approved of the spy organization and continued my work on its behalf."

Ozaki seems to have found Kawai reliable and used him mostly for information on Japanese nationalist organizations and secret societies. But Sorge's other chief Japanese assistant Miyagi, the artist from California, did not share Ozaki's opinion of him. He complained that Kawai was a "China adventurer," constantly out of work, and that "whenever he was short of money he ran to Ozaki who gave him cash." And he added, "Because of Ozaki's important position and the high calibre of the men who called on him, I thought it might embarrass Ozaki to have Kawai dropping into his office. After consulting Sorge, I suggested that henceforth I look after Kawai; Sorge approved and told me to train the man to work for me. I gave him 60 to 100 yen (about $10) every month. By May 1940 I had discovered that Kawai had no firm convictions so I sent him back to Ozaki. I could not trust Kawai fully because the standard of his comprehension of communism was low and because his private life was scandalous . . . the man hated work."

Communism was the common motive of all Sorge's spies. They were all either party members, or fellow-travellers so devoted to the party that it made no difference. In some cases, like Miyagi, they had deliberately become secret members and did not hold party cards.

The one exception was Akiyama Kosi, the only person in the spy-ring whose sole motive was money. Akiyama was a man in his forties who had spent sixteen years of his life in the United States. When he returned to Tokyo in 1933, he was out of work until he met Miyagi. "Of course," Miyagi commented later, "Akiyama knew I was a communist, but he never fully understood how secret or important my work was." And he added, "Akiyama was not a suitable kind of man for intelligence work. . . . He was not interested in social problems." But he was an adequate and willing translator and for want of a better, Miyagi, after consulting Sorge, employed him regularly for that work.

There was never any practical difficulty about the payment of members of the spy-ring. Moscow kept Sorge reasonably well financed. Over five years, he received altogether about 40,000 dollars which, at that time, meant that he could spend the equivalent of about $600 a month. But this money was only to cover expenses, not to provide salaries for his spies. Some of them were given small regular payments, but others, like Ozaki, never drew a penny: in fact Ozaki financed some of the minor agents out of his own pocket. Like all experienced espionage leaders, Sorge realized that the best spies were people who thought of themselves as idealists. Perhaps that was the reason why he told none of his Japanese recruits, not even Ozaki, that their real master was the Russian Military Intelligence. Though to Sorge himself Russia and the cause of communism were identical, he felt that to be asked to work for an agency of the Russian Government would appeal less to them than "service to the party" or to the Comintern.

From this point of view Mizuno Shige was one of his soundest men. Mizuno was a young research worker who had become an active Communist Party member while he was still at school. He had first met both Ozaki and Sorge in Shanghai where he was later arrested by the police as a communist agitator and deported to Japan. He was arrested again in Tokyo in 1936 on a charge of attempting to reorganize the Japanese Communist Party. But the police had prepared their case badly and he was soon released. He joined the Tokyo spy-ring in 1937, and worked under Miyagi, sending in reports about general social and political questions, nationalist organizations and the movement and equipment of troops.

On minor military matters, however, the ring's best source of information was a thirty-year-old corporal named Koshiro Yoshinobu who had served in the Japanese invasion of Manchuria, in the China war, and during the fighting against Red Army units, which lasted for some weeks in the summer of 1937, on the Russian-Manchurian frontier. In May 1939 a neighbor introduced him to Miyagi. As with other potential spies, Miyagi first asked for his life story, which was then sent by wireless to Moscow. There was no objection to his use, and Miyagi proceeded to recruit him. Miyagi afterwards described their preliminary conversation. "I said: 'If a war should break out between Russia and Japan it would mean a great sacrifice not only on the part of the farmers and laborers of both countries, but also on the part of the whole Japanese people. To avoid such a tragedy, that is to say a Russo-Japanese war, I am sending various data on the situation to the Comintern.' I asked Koshiro if he would help me by telling what he knew about the army and by obtaining military information from his friends. I told him that he would be paid. Koshiro did not say clearly whether he would help; he only smiled and replied that he did not know many secret matters.

He declared that I did not have to worry about money because he had savings."

Despite his early diffidence, however, Koshiro gave a great deal of secret information to Miyagi on defense plans in Manchuria, the location and equipment of troops, mobilization arrangements and the quality of various weapons. He also stole secret army and air force manuals and other military publications. Miyagi hoped to place him where he could be still more useful. "I thought it would be convenient to have him employed in some office where he would have access to military information. I thought the War Ministry, if possible the Mobilization Bureau, would be a good place, but before I could arrange it, he found a job. . . ." Sorge himself thought highly of this man; he described him a "a genuine collaborator" and, curious to know him personally, met him once or twice at restaurants in Tokyo.

Among the members of the spy-ring, there were two Japanese women. One was the 48-year-old divorced wife of a Christian cleric who had become the mistress of a Communist Party leader, had joined the party herself in 1927, and was appointed a member of a district committee. With other communist leaders, she was in prison for five years until 1934 and, just before her release, had signed a recantation. But this was only a maneuver. In 1936 she met Miyagi, who told her he was a Cominform agent and asked her help. She joined the spy-ring and began to collect information mostly on political subjects. Her name was Kuzumi Fusako.

The second woman in the spy-ring was Kitabayashi Tomo, an old friend of Miyagi; he had lived in her house in Los Angeles with his wife after their marriage. Mrs. Kitabayashi had spent many years in America with her husband and had become a member of the Communist Party there. But in 1936 she had been converted to the

Seventh Day Adventist Church and had joined the Women's Christian Temperance Union. She returned to Japan in 1936 and her husband joined her three years later. Soon after her arrival, Miyagi asked her to help him in his spy work. As her main source of information seems to have been the sewing classes at the Seventh Day Adventist Church, it was a strange request. It was also fatal. But Miyagi could hardly have foreseen that, in the end, it would be his old friend and former landlady from California, Mrs. Kitabayashi, who would destroy the whole of the Sorge spy-ring.

★   ★   ★

To recruit these and the other Japanese spies took Sorge and his assistants several years. Some of them only joined the ring towards the end. Meanwhile, he himself had been busy building up his own position with the German Embassy. Apart from the introductions which he brought from German diplomats whom he had known in China to members of the Tokyo staff, Sorge also had one very valuable personal connection. Years before in Germany, he had known a certain architect and his wife. This woman was now married to one of the Assistant Military Attachés. He revived the acquaintance and soon became very friendly with the new husband.

Lieutenant-Colonel Eugen von Ott was an efficient, loyal German officer. But it was no great secret that neither he nor his wife were particularly enthusiastic Nazis. It was even suggested that he might have been posted to Japan by sympathetic superiors who were anxious to get him out of range of political purges in the German army. In the Embassy, however, most of his colleagues were certainly supporters of the Hitler government and some of them doubtless kept von Ott under observation. He must have passed their scrutiny, for he was promoted, was appointed Military Attaché and then, at the end of 1935, became Ambassador and a Major-General. Perhaps it suited the German Government to have in Tokyo a man not too closely identified with the Nazi racial theories. At all events, whatever his private views, there is no doubt that Major-General von Ott served his government with loyalty and sincerity while he was in Japan.

Sorge impressed von Ott by his remarkable knowledge of Japanese affairs, and by his apparent discretion. Gradually other members of the Embassy also began to find Sorge useful as an informant and adviser. They started to show him official documents and to consult him about their dispatches to Berlin. Soon he was attending conferences in the Embassy, breakfasting regularly with the Ambassador, and being allowed to see the most confidential files. When war began he was invited to join the Embassy Press Office, and became the Ambassador's intimate adviser.

Thus Sorge's spy-ring was completed. Through Ozaki, he had information from the highest Japanese official circles. He himself had access to the secrets shared between Germany and Japan. De Voukelitch (who had added a post with the official French news agency to his assignments) provided information from the French Embassy and from the foreign press. And Ozaki and Miyagi between them ran a network of local spies. The ring, in fact, was admirably organized to meet the needs of the Russian Military Intelligence. From the beginning, there was only one weak link. To put that right Sorge went to Moscow early in 1935.

End of a Mission

★

Sorge travelled to Moscow by the same route that he had taken to come to Tokyo two years before; he went across the United States and through Berlin. For part of the journey, he used his own German passport; but in New York a Soviet contact-man gave him a second, forged passport which he used between Germany and Russia. It was an old document and had once belonged to an Austrian citizen with a long name which Sorge found difficult to remember; but the description and photograph were now of him. This use of double passports was familiar to him. Its purpose was to conceal his visit to Russia. Telltale Czechoslovak, Polish and Russian entry and exit visas appeared only on the forged passport which he destroyed before leaving Europe.

Sorge's "cover story" for the journey was that he had to renew his contracts with the newspapers he represented in Japan. The real reason for it was to have a general discussion of his work with his masters in Moscow and to arrange for a replacement for his incompetent wireless operator *Bernhardt*. He found that the head of the Russian Military Intelligence had changed during his absence. General Beldin had gone and another party veteran named Ulitsky had taken over. The new chief, however, was as friendly as his predecessor and equally impressed by the dangers of Sorge's job. He, too, urged Sorge to take his time in Tokyo and not to run unnecessary risks. He approved Sorge's scheme of gaining the confidence of the German Embassy, and was cooperative in finding him a new wireless operator.

The man for whom Sorge asked was Max Klausen, like himself a German and a Communist Party member, who had joined the Russian Military Intelligence in 1929. He was a specialist in secret wireless communications and he had worked for some months for Sorge in Shanghai. One report says that after his Shanghai assignment, Klausen was recalled to Moscow in 1933 and spent two years in disgrace and exile in one of the Volga German Soviet republics. This was, in fact, the period of the first Soviet purges when many party members and officials suddenly disappeared. At all events, Klausen reappeared in Moscow in the summer of 1935, met Sorge again and eagerly agreed to work with him in Tokyo. "From childhood," he afterwards said, "I had heard nothing but evil of Japan. I detested especially Japan's invasion of Manchuria. Therefore I gladly consented to go and work for Sorge there."

Klausen was a heavy, bull-headed German; an uneducated but able man. He was the son of a poor shopkeeper, and his mother had died when he was three. He was later apprenticed to a blacksmith and was called up in 1917 into the German army signal corps. Here he had his first experience of wireless. In 1921 he went to sea from Hamburg as a wireless operator, and a year later joined the new communist-dominated German Seamen's Union. The German political and economic crises of the 1920's impressed him deeply. "I came to feel," said Klausen later, "that the only doctrine which could save the German people from their misery was communism. When I visited Soviet

Russia aboard the S.S. *Neptune* and saw the fine equipment of Russian industry, I became firmly convinced that communism would promote the happiest society in the world." On his return to Hamburg from the voyage in 1927 he joined the German Communist Party, after a probationary period of six months while he was watched by party leaders. Only one year later, he was approached by a Soviet agent and asked if he would work as a wireless operator for an "international espionage organization." He agreed, went to Moscow and joined the Russian Military Intelligence in February 1929. After a short training he was sent out to China.

It was there that he met the woman who later became his wife. Anna Wallenius was a White Russian, the widow of a Finnish business man and the sister-in-law of a prominent Finnish general. Though she married Klausen in 1936, and was afterwards herself used by Sorge in Tokyo—as a courier and for other small jobs —she detested her husband's politics and his spy-work and resolutely refused to have a child by him so long as he was working for Russia.

In September 1935, Klausen left Moscow for Japan. He was given 1,800 dollars and three passports in three different names: one Italian, one Canadian and one, his own, German. He went through Leningrad, Helsinki and Stockholm to Le Havre where, with an American seaman's certificate he had bought in Sweden, he sailed on the S.S. *Boston* for New York. There he booked in, as instructed, at the Lincoln Hotel (where Sorge had stayed two years before) and was visited, like Sorge, by an American contact-man. He reached Tokyo in November and on the day of his arrival was introduced to Sorge, quite by chance, in the German club. This saved them from the trouble of going through the com-

plicated arrangements for meeting which had been prepared in Moscow.

Klausen's first task was to scrap *Bernhardt's* transmitter and to build a new set, making some of the parts
himself and buying others from shops along the Ginza.
Meanwhile, he set up an import-export business as
cover for his presence in Tokyo. But this failed and he
then established, with capital provided by Sorge, the
firm of M. Klausen Shokai which made and sold equipment for blue-prints and fluorescent plates. He used
good German material and his company soon began to
make money. Big Japanese firms, munitions factories
and the army and navy became his customers, and by
February 1941 he was able to reorganize M. Klausen
Shokai as a joint stock company with a large capital
and open a Manchurian branch in Mukden. In the end
his growing wealth began to affect his communist convictions, but meanwhile the business provided excellent
cover for the financial transactions of the spy-ring and
made it less necessary to use couriers for supplying
funds.

★   ★   ★

After his return from Moscow, Sorge began to intensify the work of the ring. His chief task was always to
report on any development which might affect the
security of the Soviet Union. For this reason he was
particularly interested in the state of the Japanese
armed forces and the political influence of their leaders.
In the spring of 1936, he was able to make a detailed
analysis of the effects of a mutiny of the army in Tokyo
which resulted in the overthrow of the Government and
an increase in the power of the Japanese militarists. His
report was not only welcomed in Moscow but a version

of it helped to increase his growing prestige in the German Embassy.

Shortly afterwards a Soviet General fled from Siberia and took refuge with the Japanese Kwantung army. He was brought to Tokyo for interrogation, and the Japanese General Staff was delighted with his information about Siberia, Mongolia and the dispositions of the Far Eastern Red Army. They informed the German Embassy and a staff officer was sent from Berlin to examine the Russian General. Sorge was allowed to borrow his report, photographed it and sent the film to Moscow. The information it contained was probably of great use to the Russians when heavy fighting broke out with the Japanese on the Manchurian frontier in the summer of 1937, for they now knew just what the fugitive had told the Japanese and were able to change the disposition of their Far Eastern troops. In the fighting, Japanese losses were extremely heavy.

By now, Prince Konoye had become Prime Minister and, for the next two years while he was in office, Ozaki's political reports, combined with Sorge's own information from the German Embassy and a mass of material from the other members of the spy-ring, enabled him to keep Moscow particularly well informed on Japanese strength and intentions. Then the second world war broke out and Sorge's assignment became even more important. Despite the Nazi-Soviet pact—which the Japanese considered a gross betrayal of their own Anti-Comintern Treaty with Germany and which had resulted in the resignation of the Japanese Government—Hitler was at pains to keep what influence he could in Tokyo. Well before his attack on Russia, senior German officers began to arrive for discussions with the Japanese General Staff of possible future military co-operation. They even prepared a plan for a Japanese attack on Singapore not unlike the operation which eventually took place. At some of these military discussions, Sorge himself was present.

In March of 1941, Prince Konoye, who had again become Prime Minister, sent his Foreign Minister, Matsuoka, on a tour to Europe: he visited Berlin, Rome and Moscow. Between them, Ozaki and Sorge were able to provide the Russians with a detailed analysis of the Japanese Government's instructions to Matsuoka and of German expectations. To the annoyance of the Germans, Matsuoka returned from his journey with a treaty of neutrality between Russia and Japan. Sorge, however, was not surprised. He had already become convinced that Japan would not attack Russia. But Moscow, despite the treaty, remained intensely suspicious of Japanese plans.

For a time, however, Sorge turned his main attention to another topic: the German danger. At the end of April 1941, he reported that 150 divisions of the Wehrmacht were being concentrated near the Russian border, and that the German General Staff expected that Leningrad would fall within two months of the start of operations. In May, he learned at the Embassy of the flight of Hess to Britain and was told that this was Hitler's last effort to make peace with the West before turning on Russia. He signalled a report to Moscow with the comment that a German attack now seemed imminent. The Russian Government was getting similar but less detailed warnings from other sources. A few days before the attack began, Sorge was told by a senior German officer who had just arrived from Berlin that the date had been fixed for June 20th. Meanwhile the Military Attaché told him that 175 divisions were now ready on the frontier. The invasion actually began two days after the date Sorge had reported.

For the Russians, it now became vitally important to know whether or not the Japanese would be persuaded to open a second front against them in the East. Early in July Sorge reported that, at a conference before the throne, it had been decided that Japan would press on with a policy of expansion towards the South but that she might declare war on Russia if the German invasion went well. A few days later, he learned from the Ambassador and other sources that the Japanese army's enthusiasm for an attack on Russia was waning, and that it would only take place if the Germans first captured Leningrad and Moscow and reached the Volga.

In August, the Japanese mobilized 1,300,000 soldiers and the Russian Government again became intensely nervous. But Sorge was able to assure his masters that there would definitely be no war against Russia that year. From the reports of Ozaki, Miyagi, Koshiro and other members of his ring, he knew that only one-third of the newly mobilized divisions had gone to Manchuria, and that they were sent there after August 15th, which was too late for an offensive before the winter. "Therefore," Sorge concluded, "Japan will not fight Russia but challenge America and England in the South." This view was confirmed in October when Ozaki gave him a carbon copy of a confidential memorandum from the Japanese Admiralty to Prince Konoye giving details of the Navy's readiness to attack American possessions in the Pacific. On October 15th, Sorge sent a final message about the negotiations then going on between the United States and Japan. He predicted that war in the Pacific was inevitable if the United States Government refused to compromise.

All this information must greatly have reassured the Russians about their own position. It would also have been of immense value to Britain and America had the

Russians passed it on. They did not do so. The Japanese
negotiators were actually in the office of Secretary of
State Hull on the day, less than two months later,
when the news reached Washington of the surprise attack on Pearl Harbor.

★   ★   ★

Sorge's assignment in Tokyo was, of course, to provide secret information. "I was strictly forbidden by
Moscow," he said later, "to engage in any non-intelli-
gence activity." And he added, "This ban meant that
my group and I were not allowed to make the least
attempt to exercise any political influence on any persons or group of persons. We obeyed it faithfully, with
one exception. . . ." The exception was that, during
the mounting tension after the outbreak of the Soviet-
German war, he himself worked on the Germans in the
Embassy, and encouraged Ozaki to work on Prince
Konoye's circle, to convince them of the dangers of a
Japanese attack on Russia. According to Sorge, this was
the argument that Ozaki used: "The Soviet Union has
no intention whatsoever of fighting Japan. . . . It
would be a short-sighted and mistaken view for Japan
to attack Russia. . . . The United States and Britain
would very likely welcome such a Japanese embroil-
ment with open arms and seize the opportunity to strike
at the nation after her oil and iron reserves were de-
pleted. . . . Should Japan aspire to further expansion
elsewhere than in China, the Southern area alone would
be worth going into, for there Japan would find the
critical resources so essential to her wartime economy,
and there she would confront the true enemy blocking
her bid for a place in the sun." Sorge commented of
Ozaki, "He was confident that if he took a strong stand
against a Soviet-Japanese war in the Konoye group he

could turn Japan's expansion policy south." Perhaps
Sorge over-estimated his assistant's influence. But Japan
did turn south against the United States and Britain,
and the reasons for her doing so—advocated by an
agent of the Russian Government, then Britain's ally—
are interesting in themselves.

★   ★   ★

Normally, Sorge himself was in direct touch with
only four members of his ring: Klausen, de Voukelitch,
Ozaki and Miyagi. At first he met them at frequent intervals in public places—the *Rheingold,* the *Fledermaus,*
Lohmeyer's and other Tokyo restaurants and bars—and
let it be understood that they were personal friends.
After 1940, when police surveillance became more
strict, they usually met in secret, often in Sorge's house,
where he lived alone. They took elaborate precautions
to make sure that they were not followed, changing
cabs at distant addresses and watching for Sorge's
safety signal, a light on the porch, before entering his
house.

Meanwhile, travel to China had become more difficult and for the first time some of the "mail" to and
from Moscow began to pass through the Soviet Embassy in Tokyo. When Sorge sent a wireless message in
1939 asking for a contact-man to meet Klausen in
Tokyo, he received the cryptic answer: *Two tickets
with higher numbers for Fritz. One with a smaller number for our contact-man.* A few days later, Klausen
found two tickets for the Imperial Theater in his mail
box at the Tokyo Central Post Office. He took his wife
with him to the performance and sat in the lower numbered seat. In the darkness, after recognition signals
had been exchanged, he passed his neighbor a package
containing thirty-eight rolls of microfilm and was given,

in return, 5,000 dollars. Klausen's neighbor was the Soviet Consul Vutokevitch. In April 1941, a second meeting took place at a theater. Shortly afterwards Vutokevitch returned to Russia and his place as contact-man was taken by another Soviet Embassy official, Viktor Zaitsev. So far as is known these brief "mail-drop" meetings were the only direct contact the Sorge spy-ring ever had with Russians in Japan.

The care taken to avoid giving the slightest cause for suspicion to the Japanese police was entirely successful. Sorge and his chief associates were well known to the authorities, who readily accepted them at their face value: Sorge the temporary diplomat, de Voukelitch the journalist, Ozaki the government adviser, Miyagi the artist, Klausen the businessman and so on. But Klausen, in particular, had a number of awkward moments. He was specially vulnerable, of course, because it was he who had charge of the most obvious and compromising secret: the wireless transmitter. Twice he was stopped by police while he was moving it from one house to another, but on each occasion it was merely a routine check and the big black brief-case in which he hid the transmitter was not examined. Once he lost, in a taxi, a copy of one of Sorge's reports for Moscow. It was never recovered, but there were no repercussions. His worst scare was not long after his arrival. Having built his new transmitter, he scrapped *Bernhardt's* old equipment. His problem then was how to dispose of it. Dressed as hikers, he and de Voukelitch travelled out to Lake Yamanaka in the country some miles from Tokyo, with the old wireless parts packed into two knapsacks. On arrival, they called at a hotel. The hotel servants helping them off with their knapsacks became suspicious of the weight and asked what they contained. "Bottles of beer," was Klausen's rather improbable reply. Afraid that the servants might report them to the police, Klausen hired a boat, hurriedly rowed to the middle of the lake and, with great relief, dropped the dangerous equipment into the water. When he heard about this afterwards Sorge commented dryly, "You should have got rid of it in Tokyo instead of going so far away."

Apart from the special risks he ran as wireless operator, Klausen's enthusiasm for his spy-work and for the cause he served began to be affected by his growing wealth, and perhaps also by his wife's continued disapproval. From April until August 1940 he had also been kept to his bed by trouble with his heart. From the end of that year he began to cut down on his transmissions to *Wiesbaden*, and during 1941 deliberately suppressed abut two-thirds of the messages Sorge gave him. He blamed "atmospherics" and Sorge did not suspect him. In July, Sorge gave him the wavelengths for a new relay station with which he was to communicate as well as *Wiesbaden*, but Klausen never used them.

By October of 1941, Sorge considered that his mission was virtually completed. For eight years he had served the Russians from Tokyo and their chief question had been answered: there would be no Japanese attack. He believed that from now on he could do more valuable work in Germany and drafted a message to Moscow suggesting that he should be transferred. The message was never sent. By that time the Japanese police were at last on Sorge's track.

★   ★   ★

The spy-ring was exposed, and Sorge himself caught, through no mistake of his. Their methods of working and their security precautions had been as perfect as anyone could make them. Strangely, it was a leading

Japanese communist, a man whom Sorge had never met and who, after the war, became a prominent member of the party's Central Committee, who was responsible for his downfall. In 1941, Ito Ritsu was twenty-nine and was employed in the Tokyo office of the South Manchurian Railway. In June he was arrested on suspicion of secret communist activity, and after interrogation by Tokyo police officers, made a full confession, recanted his communism and began to implicate other people. Among others, he named Mrs. Kitabayashi as a probable spy. His reasons for doing so are not fully known, but it seems possible that he considered her a traitor and denounced her in revenge. He knew her as a former communist who had lately severed all connection with the party.

The police began to watch Mrs. Kitabayashi, but at first found no evidence against her and did not arrest her until September 28th. She denied spying herself, but named the artist Miyagi as a communist spy. Miyagi was arrested on October 13th but vigorously denied all accusations. The police searched his house and in it found one compromising object: an English translation of a secret paper stolen from the office of the South Manchurian Railway. The police renewed their interrogations and Miyagi attempted to commit suicide by jumping from a window on the second floor of the Tsukiji police station. Policemen jumped after him and brought him back uninjured. He then admitted that he was working for an important spy-ring and said that Ozaki was his chief contact with it. The police now hesitated. Ozaki was a prominent man on close terms with the Prime Minister himself. They began to doubt Miyagi's statements and feared awkward repercussions. Then they found new evidence pointing to suspicious relations between Ozaki and several foreigners, including Dr. Sorge. Ozaki was arrested on October 15th, was interrogated at the Meguro police station, and confessed on the same day. Sorge's house was put under observation.

On October 18th, by a coincidence, Prince Konoye's government resigned. That morning, a few moments after a member of the German Embassy had left his house, Sorge was arrested. The arrests of de Voukelitch and Max and Anna Klausen took place at the same time. A search of Klausen's house revealed the wireless transmitter, coded signals and messages waiting to be coded.

Sorge was taken first to the Toriisaka police station near his home and then moved, like the other suspects, to the Tokyo Detention Prison at Sugamo. They were interrogated separately and the whole investigation was carried out in secret. At first Sorge vigorously insisted that he was a Nazi, a high adviser to the German Embassy, and knew nothing whatever about Soviet spies. But when he was told that Klausen had admitted spying for the Red Army, and that de Voukelitch had said he was an agent of the Cominform, and was shown evidence of the confessions of Miyagi and Ozaki, his attitude changed. At four o'clock on a Saturday afternoon a week after his arrest, an investigator and a policeman went to look at him to see if his health would stand further interrogation. He was, the Japanese official in charge of the investigation said, "very exhausted." He asked for a piece of paper and wrote on it twelve words: "I have been an international communist since 1925 and I am still." He then threw off his coat and said, "This is the first time that I was beaten."

Meanwhile Sorge's arrest had caused consternation at the German Embassy, which was demanding explanations and pressing for his immediate release. The Ambassador was furious, complained to the new Prime

Minister and asked the Minister of Justice for an immediate interview with Sorge. The police also feared protests from the Japanese General Staff. They were greatly relieved, and a little surprised, that Sorge confessed so quickly.

Soon afterwards General von Ott came to see Sorge, accompanied by two members of his staff. What passed at the interview has never been revealed. Von Ott emerged completely stunned, said that he would drop his protests, asked the police to speed up the investigations and requested a copy of their report. He informed Berlin what had happened, and it was apparently only then that the records of Sorge's early life were turned up by the Gestapo. Von Ott himself was replaced soon afterwards. Unable to travel to Germany, he went to Peking, and did not return to Tokyo until after the Japanese surrender in 1945.

Meanwhile the investigations proceeded slowly and in secret. The Japanese police were in no hurry. Sorge's own interrogations were completed in June 1942 and, by that time, thirty-five suspects had been arrested. Sorge himself made a detailed explanation, some of which he typed out on his own typewriter which had been brought to him from his home. He discussed his early life, his reasons for becoming a communist, how he joined the Russian Military Intelligence, his relations with the German Embassy, and the way he ran the spy-ring.

Why Sorge spoke so freely is something of a puzzle. He seemed to be anxious to emphasize his own importance and his high standing with the Russian Government. He claimed that he held the rank of Colonel in the Red Army. Probably the explanation was that he felt his mission had been successfully completed and nothing of value would be lost if the Japanese now

learned his secrets. He may also have believed that so
long as Japan and the Soviet Union were at peace
there was a chance that by a diplomatic démarche Moscow might secure his deportation to Russia. The Japanese Government did in fact seem to have been influenced by the possibility of repercussions on their
relations with the Russians. Except for one brief announcement in the press in May 1942, they kept the
investigations secret.

★   ★   ★

The members of the ring were tried separately in
secret. Thirteen were sentenced to imprisonment: Klausen and de Voukelitch for life; Kawai, Koshiro, Akiyama, Mizuno and Mrs. Kitabayashi for terms ranging
from seven to ten years. Anna Klausen got three years.
Sorge himself and Ozaki were sentenced to be hanged.
For some reason—perhaps ill-treatment and the state of
his health which had always been bad—Miyagi received no sentence and like several others, including
de Voukelitch, died in jail. Sorge and Ozaki both appealed to the Supreme Court. Sorge's appeal was dismissed in January and Ozaki's in April 1944. They were
hanged in Sugamo prison on the morning of November
7th. Both maintained their courage and dignity to the
end. One fellow-prisoner had this to say of Sorge: "My
last recollection of him was in May 1942 when I got a
glimpse of him going into the exercise pen at Sugamo
prison. At that time, of course, he had been under
arrest and subject to constant interrogation of the
severest kind over many months. . . . I can only record that at this time they had certainly not got him
down. His head was up and he walked firmly and with
that sort of dignity to which all of us prisoners aspired
but of which we so often fell short under pressure of

events. I remember feeling very strongly that, whatever he was up to, he was a very gallant fellow."

Ten months after the deaths of Sorge and Ozaki, the
American army occupied Japan. The surviving mem-
bers of the Sorge spy-ring were released. They included
Klausen and his wife, Kawai, Koshiro, Akiyama and
Mrs. Kitabayashi. In February 1946, the Klausens were
reported to have gone to Russia with the help of the
Soviet mission in Tokyo.

From Russia there has been no comment on the case
of Dr. Richard Sorge. When, after the war, a defense
lawyer attempted to mention it before an allied military
tribunal in Tokyo, the Russian prosecutor, General
Vasiliev, entered fifteen separate objections to keep it
off the record.

Meanwhile, however, Sorge's work was not without
its sequels in Japan. In December 1952, seven Japanese
were sentenced for infringements against the wave-
length laws (the new Japanese legal code provided no
penalties for spying); one of them, a former prisoner of
war from Russia, was alleged to have sent more than
eighty coded messages since 1948. They were described
as "the successors of Dr. Sorge."

The Canadian Spies

Dr. Richard Sorge spied for Russia in a hostile country while a world war was being prepared and fought. Except that he was a German, not a Russian, his own role was not unlike that of other spies working for other governments at the time —though the position of the Japanese communists who served him was different.

But Colonel Zabotin's Canadian communists spied for Russia against their own country while that country was Russia's fighting ally.

This was the first big Russian spy case to be made public in recent years. Non-communist opinion throughout the world was stunned by the story. And there were serious repercussions on the relations of the democratic Powers with Russia.

The account which follows is longer and more detailed than some of the other cases in this book. It has a special interest because it is based on facts revealed by the very Russians who controlled the spy-ring—by its chief, Zabotin himself, and his assistants, Lieutenant-Colonel Motinov, Major Rogov and their colleagues in their reports and files, and by the cipher clerk who handled all the messages exchanged with Moscow—as well as by many of their Canadian spies.

As in the other cases, all the spies but a few, minor characters, were communists, and communism was the motive which made them spy. The Communist Party played an indispensable part in the setting up and running of the spy-ring.

If Zabotin's cipher clerk had not broken with his masters, that spy-ring might never have been exposed. But, even so, its exposure gives only one brief glance at one small part of the whole Russian spy system. In Canada alone, there were several other independent Russian spy-rings working at that time. Zabotin himself hinted that there were nine; the Canadian Government found evidence of four. About them, nothing is publicly known.

V

The Genial Colonel

★

There was nothing at all strange about the arrival of
the new Soviet Military Attaché in Ottawa in June 1943.
Some weeks before, the Russian Legation had officially
notified the Canadian Government of the appointment
of Colonel Nicolai Zabotin. He came with his Secretary,
Major Romanov, and an assistant, Igor Gouzenko. The
flight from Moscow, across Siberia, the Arctic and the
wastes of Northern Canada, was long and uneventful.
But the three Russians enjoyed their journey. Colonel
Zabotin himself—at least, when he wanted to be pleasant
—was an entertaining companion. A tall, handsome artillery officer, with greying, wavy hair, and a booming, self-
confident manner, he had held his commission in the
Red Army for 19 years, and his anecdotes of service life,
especially of his tour of duty in Mongolia, made entertaining hearing. The Colonel was clearly looking forward
to his new assignment, and he did his best to put his
two travelling companions at their ease: Romanov, the
usually quiet and efficient Staff Officer, whose only fault
was a prodigious desire for drink without a correspond-
ing ability to carry it; and Gouzenko, the young Red
Army lieutenant, still feeling slightly awkward in his
new official status as a civilian clerk.

For all three, this was to be the first taste of life and
work outside the frontiers of the Soviet Union. Despite

the detailed briefing, which they had been given at head-quarters in Moscow before leaving, they were still filled with curiosity, and a good deal of apprehension, about "capitalist" Canada. For though they had been given full, routine instructions on the behavior of Soviet citizens abroad, and had been warned that only in exceptional circumstances could any foreigner be trusted, the Moscow briefing had thrown little light on what Canada and Canadians were really like. A large part of it, in fact, had been devoted to the three Russians themselves. Like other Soviet officials employed abroad on the type of work that they were going to do, each of them had been given an elaborate and entirely fictitious life story to memorize before he left Russia. This biographical "legend" bore no relation to the real facts of their lives. Its purpose was to make it impossible for the Canadian Government, to whom they were accredited, to check up —through the Canadian Legation in Moscow or in any other way—on their earlier careers.

The Colonel's early impressions of Canada were very pleasant. Young Gouzenko was so disconcerted by his first greeting from a Canadian airman when their aircraft landed—"Hi-ya, pal. How's Joe?"—that it took him several seconds to realize that this irreverent inquiry referred to Generalissimo Stalin. He then dutifully followed the official instruction laid down for such a situation, froze up and pretended to speak no English. But to the Colonel, the easy manner and obvious friendliness of the Canadians seemed a good omen for his future work. Russia at this time was at the height of her popularity in Canada. The exploits of the Red Army were widely publicized in the Canadian press. Official policy favored the friendliest possible relations with the Soviet ally. And Russians, above all Russian officers in uniform, were a rarity in Ottawa. So as soon as he began to make his first personal contacts in the capital, the Colonel was at once overwhelmed with invitations. Friendly Canadians eagerly competed in their efforts to help him "to get to know us." On the official level, too, he found Colonel Jenkins and his liaison officers at National Defense Headquarters delighted to cooperate with the new Soviet Military Attaché. They readily gave him whatever information he asked for and promptly arranged visits to those military establishments he said he wished to see. In fact, during the whole of his stay in Ottawa they never refused a single official request from Colonel Zabotin. They were surprised only that he asked so little.

To these free and friendly relations with his Canadian hosts and colleagues the atmosphere inside the Soviet Legation provided a sharp contrast. At the time of his arrival, the Military Attaché's Department was still in the main Legation building at 285 Charlotte Street. It was here, in the big Victorian, slate-roofed, red-brick house with the high, white porches, that Zabotin met his new colleagues.

Among them he found little reflection of the prevailing enthusiasm for the war-time alliance between Russia and the Western Powers. Disciplined and cynical—in their spoken thoughts at least—they all echoed the approved Stalinist line. Cooperation with some of the capitalist countries had become a temporary necessity, they said, after Hitler had betrayed his pact with Stalin and attacked the Soviet Union on June 22nd, 1941. On that date the world war had abruptly ceased to be a "predatory conspiracy of imperialist aggressors" and had become a "just peoples' struggle for independence and liberation." For the time being, therefore, the alliance was necessary and useful. Among other benefits, it was providing Russia with vast quantities of supplies and arms, many of them from Canada. But this situation would not last. The teachings of Marx and Lenin inexorably proved that a final conflict between communist and non-comunist countries was inevitable, and that, in that conflict, non-communist society would perish. Loyal Soviet officials must face up to these realities. A third world war would come—a war in which Canada, too, would be an enemy. If simple, naïve Canadians did not understand that elementary fact, so much the worse for them. But the Soviet Union must work for the future as well as for the present. Such were the views expressed by Colonel Zabotin's colleagues inside the precincts of the Legation. Outside, of course, they voiced quite different sentiments, designed to exploit the prevailing goodwill toward Russia.

To an outsider, glancing at the pages of the Ottawa diplomatic list, the staff of the Soviet Legation seemed to follow the accepted pattern. It looked just like any other foreign mission. Headed by His Excellency Minister Feodor Gousev (later replaced by Ambassador G. N. Zarubin, when the Legation was raised to the status of an Embassy in 1944), it was divided into the usual grades of Counsellors, Secretaries, Attachés and their assistants. But in practice these titles bore little relation to the actual functions of many members of the staff. In fact, the Soviet section of the diplomatic list was nothing more than an elaborate piece of camouflage to hide their real work.

The Minister himself was an exception to this strange game of bluff. He was what he appeared to be: the senior official in the Legation responsible for handling ordinary diplomatic business. But his authority over his colleagues was curiously limited. Listed in a relatively junior position on his staff, for example, was "Second Secretary and Consul" Vitali G. Pavlov. No outsider could have guessed that Pavlov used his consular duties merely as a cover for his work as chief of the Canadian network of the Soviet Secret Police, taking his orders straight from the N.K.V.D. in Moscow. Nor, for that matter, did appearances reveal that "Commercial Counsellor" Krotov had formerly worked as Assistant to Malenkov when Malenkov was head of the foreign section of the Soviet Communist Party, and that Krotov now devoted most of his working time in Ottawa to military espionage.

Likewise, in 1944, when the Legation became an Embassy, one of the new diplomats to arrive from Moscow was Second Secretary Goussarov. His official title gave no hint that Goussarov actually held a position of authority equal to that of the Ambassador himself, that he was the direct representative of the Central Committee of the Russian Communist Party, the senior party official in the Embassy, the chief of the Comintern's intelligence system in Canada, and the channel through which directives passed from Moscow to the Canadian Communist Party.

Among the more junior employees, too, there were similarly curious appointments. There was, for example, Gorshkov, the Military Attaché's "civilian chauffeur" who was actually a Red Army Captain and a trained photographic laboratory technician. There were Galkin and Goussev, nominally two "civilian doormen" and in reality a Captain and a Technical Lieutenant who compiled some of the Embassy's most secret files. There was even some mystery round the real functions of Borovkov, the chef. Rumor had it that he combined his duties in the kitchen, at which he was very skilful, with more sinister services for the N.K.V.D. There was, in fact, a general atmosphere of conspiracy among the Soviet diplomats, many of whom were doing jobs which were kept secret even from their colleagues.

Colonel Zabotin found that, apart from his own department, there were four other distinct and independent branches in the Legation. The Minister's Department worked for the Soviet Foreign Ministry; the Commercial Department for the Ministry of Foreign Trade; the Political Department for the Russian Communist Party; and Pavlov and his staff for the Ministry which controlled the N.K.V.D. Each of these departments kept its work secret from the others. It had its own direct communications with Moscow, its own cipher, and its own cipher officer. There was little exchange of information and a good deal of interdepartmental friction, in which Zabotin himself was later destined to become involved. The Minister was firmly excluded from much of what went on in his Legation, and was even forbidden to enter one part of the building.

This was the secret section which housed the cipher offices and the confidential files. It was on the second floor of the rear wing and had once been the servants' quarters. Here, in Room 12, was the office of young Gouzenko, the Colonel's cipher officer. Each time Gouzenko and the other authorized members of the staff wanted to enter the section, they had first to press a concealed bell-push under the banister on the stairs. Then, reaching a heavy velvet curtain, they would draw it back to uncover a massive steel door. In the door, at face level, was a small opening through which the guard on duty behind, warned by the bell, could peer to identify whoever was outside. The door would then be opened to reveal a second steel door behind. Inside was a carpeted corridor with offices opening off it. The glass in the windows was painted white, so that no one should see through, and was protected by iron bars and heavy steel shutters. A wireless at the end of the corridor played continuously during working hours to prevent talk in any of the offices being audible outside. Each office had a steel safe for documents and files, and there was an incinerator in Room 14 for destroying unwanted secret papers. There was also a second incinerator in another room, large enough, it was rumored, to destroy a human body. In fact, the security arrangements in the secret section of the Soviet Legation building left little for the imagination.

Of Colonel Zabotin's staff, only Gouzenko worked permanently in this secret wing. Here he deciphered messages from Moscow, enciphered the replies and watched over the confidential files. At first the Military Attaché's Department was small, officially consisting only of Zabotin himself, Major Romanov and Gouzenko. Unofficially there were also Krotov, the Commercial Counsellor; a Major Sokolov, who appeared on the diplomatic list as a member of the Commercial Department; a civilian First Secretary, Sergei Koudriavtzev; and Nicolai Zheveinov, the chief Ottawa correspondent of *Tass,* the Soviet News Agency. But soon additions to Zabotin's staff arrived from Moscow, until it included a dozen highly trained, carefully selected officers. Now he moved his department—except for the cipher officer —from the main Legation building to a large house standing in a garden at 14 Range Road in a different district of the city. Here he settled down to serious business.

Like the work of many of his colleagues, the Colonel's chief task had little to do with his official post. For appearances' sake, he carried out the formal duties of a Military Attaché, keeping in touch with National Defense Headquarters, attending parades and exercises, even lecturing on the Red Army to Canadian Military Schools. But his real interests were entirely different.

His chief in Moscow, Colonel-General Kouznetzov, was head of Soviet Military Intelligence. Zabotin's assignment was to develop a powerful network of Canadian spies.

Though the German armies still occupied almost all Europe and a large part of Russia, and Hitler was still defiant, Russian military espionage in Canada in 1943 was not chiefly concerned with the war then being fought. Much information relevant to the war itself the Colonel could have had simply by asking for through official channels. He rarely did so. His training taught him to distrust open sources of information. He could not believe that the alliance made the Canadian Government any less secretive or suspicious of foreigners than his own government in Moscow. Besides, the Soviet leaders were already preoccupied with the future —that future when, so their strange doctrines predicted, Russia and the West would no longer be allies but deadly enemies. So Zabotin's espionage assignment was very wide. He was mainly interested in developments which might affect the post-war strength of Canada and the Western Powers. The targets for his spies ranged from the location of airfields on the Pacific coast to Canada's post-war economics, from the forging of passports to the secrets of the atom bomb.

He found on his arrival that good foundations had already been laid for his future work. Some years before, while Russia still had no diplomatic mission in Canada, Soviet intelligence agents, operating from across the border in the United States, had established the beginnings of a Canadian military spy-ring. Early in 1942, this work had been taken over by Major Sokolov who came to Ottawa posing as an inspector of armaments which were being made for Russia under the Canadian Mutual Aid Program. At that time

Sokolov had taken his orders from an official of the Soviet Consulate in New York named Mihailov. Mihailov himself had visited Ottawa during the summer to check up on Sokolov's work. Later in 1942, when a Soviet Legation was established in Ottawa, Mihailov had handed over his Canadian responsibilities to the new First Secretary there, Sergei Koudriavtzev, who then became Sokolov's chief. But with Zabotin's arrival, both Sokolov and Koudriavtzev joined the Colonel's staff. From them he learned the details of the spy-ring which it was his duty to reorganize and expand.

★   ★   ★

At the time that Zabotin took over there were two main groups of spies working for his network. Each group was headed by a leader of the Canadian Communist Party, through whom the groups' members had been recruited. The spies included highly placed scientists, officials and officers in government departments and the services, and from them came a steady flow of stolen documents and most secret information. Their reports were sifted and collated in Ottawa, and then sent on to Moscow in cipher telegrams, by special courier, or by diplomatic bag.

All this was highly satisfactory. But it was only a beginning. Moscow now expected Colonel Zabotin to build a bigger, more efficient spy-ring with far more spectacular results. There seemed to be no reason why he should not succeed. Over the years, Soviet military intelligence had developed an exceedingly efficient espionage technique. Its headquarters in Moscow was large and well organized. Its officers, both there and abroad, were all hand-picked, carefully screened and highly trained. Its security arrangements seemed perfect. Zabotin himself had been provided with a big staff and ample funds. Besides, the experience of Sokolov and Koudriavtzev had already proved that in Canada it was not difficult to find high-grade, well-placed spies who were willing to work for Russia.

The future, in fact, looked bright as Colonel Zabotin settled down to work in his comfortable, well-guarded office at Range Road.

VI

The Ring Expands

★

In Colonel Zabotin's department, secrecy was all-important. The rules designed to protect that secrecy were comprehensive and they were rigidly enforced. Among other things, they required that no one outside the department should know anything of its operations, and that no one outside the Soviet mission should know of its existence; that its files should never leave Gouzenko's office in Room 12; that spies and their Russian contact-men should be referred to by code-names only; and that documents not in use should immediately be burned. There were also detailed instructions for the handling of spies. They covered such matters as the use of passwords and recognition signals, the procedure to be followed at secret street-corner meetings, the giving of bribes and the disposal of spies who became unreliable or suspect. To ensure that these rules and instructions were obeyed, the Military Attaché's staff was under rigorous discipline. The smallest mistake might mean immediate recall to Moscow, followed by consequences unpleasant enough to be a very adequate deterrent.

Colonel Zabotin himself was responsible for all the work of his department. It was to him that the Director of the branch of Soviet Military Intelligence which dealt with North America addressed instructions, and Zabotin personally signed all the reports and messages which were sent to Moscow. For this purpose he always used his code-name *Grant*. But the Colonel never met any of his spies himself. And much of the routine work, as well as the money paid to spies, was handled for him by the chief Assistant Military Attaché, Lieutenant-Colonel Motinov. Next in seniority came the Assistant Military Attaché (Air), Lieutenant-Colonel Rogov, followed by the two majors: Romanov, his Personal Assistant (who was eventually replaced), and Sokolov, the first organizer of the spy-ring. Then came two captains: Gorshkov and Galkin, followed by five lieutenants. There were also the three civilians, Krotov the Commercial Counsellor, Koudriavtzev the First Secretary and Zheveinov the *Tass* correspondent. Normally, none of the staff did any spying themselves, and some of them, like Gouzenko, worked only inside the office. But others, including Motinov, Rogov and Sokolov, were in direct contact with spies. Only the leading members of the spy-ring, however, were allowed to meet Russians, and even they were not allowed to know their real names. In theory, too, each Russian was supposed to be in contact with only one Canadian spy. The minor members of the ring never met a Russian and passed their information through one or more Canadian intermediaries. Some of them were only dimly aware that the Soviet mission was the channel through which their information went to Moscow.

For each Canadian in the military spy-ring, a file was kept in the steel safe in Room 12. Clipped inside the cover was a "registration sheet" bearing, in the top right corner, the spy's photograph, followed by personal details listed under six headings: surname, name and father's name; code-name; office and home addresses; place of work and position; financial status (which included an entry as to whether or not the spy took Russian money); and biographical data. In the rest of the file was kept a complete day-to-day record of the spy's instructions and performance.

Before a spy could be recruited to the ring, however, he was screened with the greatest care. The Canadian (a senior member of the ring) who had proposed him to the Russians was asked to provide a full description of him, of his work and of the kind of information he could supply, his life story and a photograph. A summary of this information was at once sent to Moscow with a request for permission to use him. Soviet Military Intelligence then checked his record both against their own files and with the N.K.V.D. and the Comintern. They made sure that he was not, as sometimes happened, already working for some other Soviet espionage organization. If inquiries showed that there was no objection to his use, the Director in Moscow would then telegraph approval to Colonel Zabotin. All the preliminaries were completed without the knowledge of the person concerned, who was often unaware that he was known to the Russians at all. Sometimes the procedure was reversed and the Director in Moscow would telegraph suggesting the name of a Canadian recruit to Colonel Zabotin. That he could do so proved that Soviet Military Intelligence had other, independent channels of information from Canada.

For expanding his organization, the Colonel had several possible sources of recruits. Of these, the Canadian Communist Party was easily the most important. Founded in secret by agents of the Comintern who came to Canada in 1921, that party had grown until its membership was larger, in proportion to the population, than the Communist Parties of Britain or the United States. Some eight out of every ten of its members were

foreign-speaking immigrants or Canadians of foreign
descent: people whose families had come to Canada
from the Ukraine, Finland, Poland, Hungary and other
European countries. The party was efficiently organized
and it was relatively rich. It owned businesses ranging
from insurance companies and cooperatives to laun-
dries, retail shops and legal firms. From these, indirectly,
it drew a large part of its funds.

Politically, the Canadian Communist Party was always fiercely militant and made no secret of its allegiance to the Soviet Union. It followed faithfully all the
changes and abrupt reversals of policy ordered by the
Comintern. For the first three years of its existence it
worked underground, covering its activities for most of
that period with a fictitious but legal "front" which it
controlled: the so-called Workers' Party. In 1924, the
Workers' Party changed its name to the Communist
Party of Canada. Seven years later, eight of its leaders
were jailed by the Government for conspiracy, inciting
to violence and other crimes. As the second world war
came nearer the Canadian communists, like their comrades in other countries, clamored loudly for effective
resistance to Nazi aggression. But one month after the
war began, they reversed this policy and launched a
violent campaign to sabotage the war effort. In reply,
the Canadian Government outlawed the party in June
1940 and ordered the detention of most of its leaders.
The party again went underground, pouring out a
stream of illegal propaganda, and some of the leaders
went into hiding. But a year later, Russia was forced
into the war. Promptly the communists again reversed
their policy, pledging vigorous support for the Government, and soon afterward the missing leaders surrendered to the police. They were released almost at once,
but the party remained illegal. So in August 1943, one

month after Colonel Zabotin's arrival in Ottawa, they set up a new "front" organization, the Labor-Progressive Party which everyone knew was simply the old Communist Party of Canada under a different name. It operated quite freely, however, contested provincial and federal elections and, in August 1943, won one seat in the Dominion Parliament.

Without the Canadian Communist Party, Colonel Zabotin's spy-ring could not have existed. The party provided him with an almost unlimited field for recruiting eager, efficient and well-placed spies. But those spies did not usually come from the rank and file. His two key men were both prominent party leaders: men well known to the Canadian public as communist agitators —and also well known to the police. Because of their reputations and their political activity, neither of them was of much use as a first-hand source of information. Except on rare occasions, neither had direct access to secrets which would interest the Russians. But as advisers and as contact-men they were invaluable. Their long communist training gave them a perfect understanding of Colonel Zabotin's requirements, and they knew exactly where to look among their comrades in the party to find him other spies.

*　　　*　　　*

According to the file in Zabotin's department, full details of the life of Sam Carr, alias Schmil Kogan, are on record in the office of the Comintern in Moscow. Born in the Ukraine, he had come to Canada in 1924 at the age of 18. A year later, as Sam Cohen, he joined the Young Communist League in Montreal, and in 1927 became a full member of the Communist Party. After ten years of activity on its behalf, interrupted by a prison sentence of which he served three years, he became the party's National Organizer. Meanwhile, during a visit to Russia in 1929, he had, according to Zabotin's file, attended a course in subversive political work at the Lenin School in Moscow. With other Canadian communist leaders he disappeared in 1940 and probably went into hiding in the United States. At the end of September 1942 he reappeared, surrendered to the police in Toronto, and was released within a fortnight, after signing formal declarations to desist from communist activity and not to communicate to "anyone whomsoever" information about the war. Only a few days later he arranged a secret meeting with Sergei Koudriavtzev, the First Secretary of the Soviet Legation, who was then in charge of the military spy-ring. By the time of Zabotin's arrival he was at the head of an active group of spies operating in Ottawa and Toronto. Apart from his work as an intermediary and recruiting agent, Carr was also a specialist in smuggling and illegal frontier crossings and in obtaining forged passports and identity papers. His Russian contact-man continued to be Koudriavtzev.

Zabotin's second key man was the Honorable Fred Rose, M.P., who as a "Labor-Progressive" candidate was elected to the Canadian House of Commons one month after Zabotin's arrival. His life story is very like that of his comrade, Carr, except that he became a spy much sooner. An entry in his file in Zabotin's office showed that before the age of seventeen he had worked for the Soviet secret police. He was born in Poland, to Russian parents named Rosenberg, and came to Canada as a 13-year-old boy in 1920. Like Carr, he became a member of the Young Communist League in 1925 and of the Communist Party in 1927. Two years later he joined the Central Executive Committee, and in 1930, like Carr, he took a course at the Lenin School in Moscow. In 1937 he joined the Central Control Commission of his party, a body whose job it was to do counter-espionage among the members. He, too, disappeared in 1940, surrendered in September 1942 and was released on October 6th, after signing undertakings like Carr.

Rose first offered to join the spy-ring while he was still in hiding in the summer of 1942. But Major Sokolov, who was then in charge, did not accept him at once because his services were also wanted by his old masters, the N.K.V.D. Sokolov's chief, Mihailov, came up from New York at that time to reorganize the ring. He outbid the N.K.V.D., got Moscow's approval to use Rose and ordered him to approach Sokolov again. This he did in September, shortly before surrendering to the police. On his release, he started work, and when Zabotin arrived next June, Rose was in charge of a group of spies in government departments. Though he too, like Carr, acted chiefly as an intermediary, he did sometimes send in his own reports, including, on one occason, an account of a secret session of the Canadian House of Commons.

Rose and Carr played leading roles in the work of the Russian military spy-ring. They were the only members who were trusted to know something of its real scope and aims. Their relations with the Russians were altogether exceptional, probably because they had both been trained in Moscow and had already spent a great part of their lives in secret work for Russia. Rose, at least, had made spying his career at a very early age; he may even have been sent to Canada specially for that purpose.

For men like these, Colonel Zabotin and his Director in Moscow were prepared to waive the usual rules of Soviet espionage. But in all ordinary cases those rules laid it down that no one publicly associated with a

Communist Party must ever be used as a spy. This meant that for the great majority of new recruits Zabotin had to draw on secret party members—the crypto-communists—and on fellow-travellers. These recruits, moreover, had to be intelligent, educated people, in positions of trust where they had access to valuable information. Fortunately for him, the Canadian Communist Party was admirably organized to produce, in large numbers, exactly this type of person.

The methodical, highly efficient system by which the party trained and developed its secret members did not exist merely to furnish spies to Colonel Zabotin. It was a big undertaking and served a wider purpose. Communist activity always needs a good supply of reliable crypto-communists to undertake such tasks as undermining trade union branches, infiltrating political movements, and setting up "front" organizations which the party controls from behind the scenes. People trained to do such work often make excellent spies.

To meet the demand for this sort of "crypto," the Canadian Communist Party deliberately discouraged certain sympathizers from becoming ordinary members. These people included students, scientific workers, teachers, professional employees and, particularly, men and women working, or likely to work, in government service. Instead of taking out party cards, they were invited to join one of a number of small study-groups which met at regular intervals in private houses in various Canadian cities. Ostensibly these groups, each numbering perhaps a dozen members, were simply informal collections of like-minded men and women drawn together by a common interest in politics and current affairs. Often new members believed them to be just that. But in fact they formed a carefully organized network of cells under the close supervision of the party.

The subjects discussed were part of a well-designed course for training militant Stalinists. The chairman of each group attended meetings with five or six chairmen from other groups for guidance and instruction. From time to time, one of the party leaders would casually drop in on a discussion, and get to know new members of the group. Afterwards his impressions would be added to the secret dossier that was quietly being compiled about each member's political development, character and capabilities.

Inevitably the time would come, perhaps after some months or years of indoctrination, when a new member of a study-group would be anxious to take a more active part in Communist Party work. He would then be advised that he could join the party, in the sense of paying a regular subscription through the chairman of his group, but that he must keep his relations with the party secret and that he would not be issued a membership card. He was also warned that he must now accept party discipline and that any hesitation in obeying orders would mean immediate expulsion.

Gradually the atmosphere of conspiracy and discipline—of secret meetings, secret acquaintances and secret loyalties—would so condition the minds of members of these cells that they would be ready to undertake any assignment from their party and to do whatever it might ask. Their integrity as Canadian citizens would be destroyed, and "loyalty to the party" would begin to take precedence over every other consideration. It was at this stage that they became potential spies. In fact, apart from Rose and Carr, and a few forgers and other "specialists" who worked for bribes, all but two of Zabotin's known spies were recruited from study-groups of this kind.

The actual approach to a cell member—the first proposal that he should spy—was, of course, a very delicate
operation. Usually it was done by a senior communist:
someone of the standing of Rose or Carr. And it was
never put bluntly. The suggestion might be made that,
from time to time, "the Party" would be interested in
a little "background information" which the cell member could pick up at work. At this stage, there would
be no mention of writing reports or stealing secret papers. Nor would anything be said about military espionage or Russians. The new spy might start simply by
telling some trusted party comrade of odd items which
he had overheard or read in his office. Sometimes he
would do so, privately, at meetings of the study-group
itself. A little later, he might be asked to watch for information on particular subjects, or to find the answers
to specific questions. Then, to start taking notes. From
there, it was only a short, easy step until, like several
of Zabotin's recruits, he was regularly handing over
whole sheaves of top-secret documents to the Russians.

What were the reactions of these study-group communists when they were first told to spy? Many of them
later tried to explain. Their explanations were often
muddled and confused. They found it hard to admit
their real feelings. In their hearts they all knew, from
the beginning, that what they were being asked to do
was illegal: a betrayal of their employers and a violation
of solemn promises to respect official secrets. Sometimes
they hesitated. "It was a struggle—it is always a struggle," one confessed. But in the end not one of them
refused. They justified their actions by persuading
themselves that they were serving some higher purpose:
"the cause of science," "international understanding,"
"allied unity," "the Party." They shut their eyes to the
simple fact that this was espionage for a foreign Power.

But all of them realized, sooner or later, that their information was going straight to Moscow.

What they did not always realize was the size of the spy-ring they were serving. "I had no idea of the scope and extent of this work," said one. "I was amazed when it became clear to me" (after his arrest). And he added: "I was trying to square myself with my ideals without a full knowledge of the position in which I really found myself."

From Colonel Zabotin's point of view, the study-group spies had many merits. They were already disciplined and used to secret work. Normal prejudices against lying, theft and treachery they scorned as childish "bourgeois morality." They spied from conviction and they were ready to take big risks. But though these men and women convinced themselves that idealism was their motive, idealism played little part in the calculations of their masters. Carefully noted in the files in Colonel Zabotin's department were penetrating observations on the frailties and failings of each. Always there was an entry about the need or desire for money. Money was no part of the original motive of this type of spy. But its use was a part of the technique of Zabotin and his colleagues. They were careful not to mention the subject too soon. They knew that such people, facing the first grave decision, would probably be more insulted than encouraged by the thought of bribes. But later they would deliberately offer money to spies who had never asked for it and did not need it: usually small sums at first, which they tactfully described as "expenses." They calculated, probably correctly, that a spy who had taken money, even against his will, would afterwards feel himself to be more deeply committed. Sometimes it was accepted without a second thought; sometimes it was angrily rejected. One spy afterwards complained that Major Sokolov "was always bringing up the question of expenses . . . but it was from our point of view a preposterous suggestion and I simply ignored it." In the end, however, this spy and his associates did take money from the Russians. But they continued to believe that their real motive was "idealistic."

Apart from these secret communists, a second source of recruits for the Colonel's ring were professional agents: men who freely admitted that their only motive was money and who took as much as they could get. But they were far less reliable than the communists and there were fewer of them. They were used only when no one else could do the job. For example, when Moscow asked Zabotin to have a Canadian passport issued for a spy in the United States, Carr arranged this for him through officials of the Ottawa Passport Office. It cost the Russians three thousand dollars. But when money was needed, it was readily produced.

Secret departments are usually well financed, and Soviet Military Intelligence was no exception. Once Zabotin spent twenty-five thousand dollars in two months for diplomatic mail alone. In order to prevent the Canadian Government noticing this heavy expenditure, his funds reached him in a roundabout way. Sometimes Canadian banknotes came in the diplomatic bag. Once he cabled to his Director: *The Ambassador has agreed to help us by giving us an amount of money from the Embassy and he proposes that the money be sent back in small sums to his address at the Embassy and to the address of the Commercial Counsellor. Small amounts might also be added to the entertainment expenses. . . .*

A third possible source of spies for Colonel Zabotin were Russians and Ukrainians living in Canada, and immigrants from other countries occupied by the Soviet Union. In their case, if other motives failed, threats of reprisals against relatives still in Europe might make them spy. But there was the disadvantage that few such people had access to information which the Russians wanted, or were qualified to help in other ways. In fact, only one of Zabotin's known spies came from this category.

But Zabotin's orders were to expand his spy-ring. Constant messages from his Director in Moscow reminded him of the need to recruit more spies. So he left no possible source of recruits untried. He looked in the most unlikely places. Even in his social contacts, the cheerful, booming Russian (who enjoyed a party and seldom refused an invitation) was always carefully watching for potential spies. There was, for example, a Colonel—a straightforward, hospitable Canadian—who had met Zabotin, Motinov and Rogov socially, and who, with his wife, had tried, he afterwards explained, "to make them feel at home in Canada, and to show them something of Canadian life." No one could have been less like a communist or a potential spy. But Motinov was ordered to prepare a plan for recruiting him and another officer to the spy-ring.

The first stage, according to Motinov's documents, was to win his confidence. Because the Colonel worked in a responsible position he had, Motinov assumed, signed the Official Secrets Act. *Therefore,* wrote the Russian, *the character of the work must be the usual one—a personal touch in conversations on various subjects beginning with oneself, one's own biography, work and daily life, at times asking them, as if for comparison, of this or that situation. . . .* Motinov then listed a series of *Questions to be clarified.* They included the life story of each man, whether he liked the service, what his relations were with his immediate superiors, and, under the heading *Personal Positive and Negative*

Sides, the following points: (*a*) *Inclination to drink, good family man;* (*b*) *Love of good times, inclination for solitude and quietness;* (*c*) *Influence of wife on his actions, independence in making decisions;* (*d*) *Circle of acquaintances and brief character sketches of them.* Then came an entry *Program for future,* followed by the words *Ideological or financial requires to be determined.*

But neither ideology nor finance could possibly have turned this officer into a Soviet spy. Zabotin soon realized that, and turned elsewhere. The Canadian Colonel himself knew nothing until afterward of Zabotin's strange reaction to his friendly hospitality.

But one failure did not deter the Soviet Military Attaché. His policy was to look everywhere, try everything. He redoubled his efforts to expand his spy-ring. And it was not long before he began to achieve astonishing results.

VII

A Mixed Bag

★

Kathleen Mary Willsher was thirty-eight. She was a quiet, ordinary-looking woman, short, dark, unattractive and a spinster. Born in England and a graduate of the London School of Economics, she had come to Canada in 1930 when she was twenty-five as a shorthand-typist in the office of the British High Commissioner. She did well in her job, was promoted several times, and by 1943 worked in the registry, where she saw and filed highly secret documents and telegrams. I believe that, years before, I had met Kathleen Willsher once or twice in London, but I remember nothing at all about her. That is not surprising, for she had never seemed in any way remarkable. Certainly in Ottawa in 1943, none of her fellow civil servants guessed that their reticent, soft-speaking colleague was a woman with a double life: a militant communist and a Soviet spy.

When Colonel Zabotin arrived in Ottawa in June of that year, one of his first tasks was to compile a detailed report on the organization of the military spy-ring as he found it when he took over from Sergei Koudriavtzev and Major Sokolov. Much of the material for that report was ready for him in the files in the steel safe in Room 12. One of those filed was labelled with the code-name *Elli*. It told a strange, rather pathetic story. A story of how skilful, calculated planning had led a

89

well-meaning, rather naïve young woman from draw-
ing-room political discussions to furtive street-corner
meetings and the theft of official secrets. *Elli* was Kathleen Willsher. She had been spying for eight years.

It was Fred Rose who undertook to "develop" Kathleen Willsher. He used the well-established study-
group technique. She was invited to join her first group
in 1934 and attended regular meetings in private homes
in Ottawa. The purpose, she was told, was to discuss
current political questions against a background of so-
called scientific Marxism. Soon she realized that the
group was closely connected with the Canadian Communist Party. From time to time, Rose came to the discussions and so she got to know him. About a year
later, he suggested that she should spy. He put it to her
in a roundabout way, saying that "the party would be
very glad to have some information sometimes" from
her office, which would be of value to it "in formulating
its program." At first his request upset her. She took a
month to make up her mind. Then she began to watch
the files in the High Commission and to report to him
on their contents. This arrangement lasted for four
years. Meanwhile, in 1936, she joined the Communist
Party as a secret member, paying her subscriptions
through the chairman of her study-group. Then the
war started and, without warning, she lost touch with
Rose. Her spying temporarily stopped.

It began again some months after Major Sokolov arrived in Canada to reorganize the military spy-ring.
The method of approach was exactly the same as
before. Late in 1942, a Miss Agatha Chapman, an
Englishwoman employed in the Bank of Canada, telephoned to her and invited her to join a second study-
group. Its leader was another civil servant, also a secret
communist, named Eric Adams. Adams acted as an in-

termediary for Sam Carr and himself later became a direct spy for the Russians. For two years Kathleen Willsher met Adams regularly at the study-group at Miss Chapman's home. There he would pass on her instructions. Usually he put to her specific questions. She would then compile the answers from the secret files at the High Commission, and report to him at the next meeting. In 1944 she was promoted by the High Commissioner and became Assistant Registrar.

Early in 1945 Adams, her contact-man, was transferred to Montreal. But their Russian masters saw no reason to change an arrangement which was working well. From then on, at intervals, Miss Chapman would telephone to Kathleen Willsher to tell her the date, time and place of the next meeting. Adams would drive over to Ottawa in his car, pick Kathleen Willsher up on some deserted, prearranged street corner, drop her again after ten or fifteen minutes when their business was finished, and drive back to Montreal. Once, on instructions from Miss Chapman, she went over to Montreal to see him, paying her four-and-a-quarter-dollar train fare out of twenty-five dollars Adams had given her for "expenses."

In this way she went on spying for another year. How much she knew of the other operations of the spy-ring is not clear. Afterwards, in her hesitating, muddled way, she insisted that her motive was to help "the Party," although she realized that Moscow was where her information went. She also understood the gravity of what she did. For though she thought of herself as a very minor servant of the Russians ("It didn't seem that I was of very great importance," she said), she fully expected, if she were discovered, to be shot. But she still continued to add her contribution of

stolen information to the dispatches and telegrams of
Colonel Zabotin.

★   ★   ★

After Kathleen Willsher, the next spy, in length of
service, in the military ring was a temporary civil servant in a Canadian Government department. Of him,
the Colonel wrote:

*Gray. Jew. Head of a Section of the Directorate for
securing war material for the allies. Taken on to work
on 1.9.42. He works well. Gives material on shells and
cannons. . . .*

Many later reports from Zabotin to Moscow confirmed that *Gray* worked well. His information mostly
concerned explosives and munitions. His Russian contact-man was Major Sokolov. To Sokolov, at frequent
intervals, *Gray* passed notes, photographs and documents, sometimes himself choosing what he knew
would interest the Russians, sometimes answering requests for particular information. *Gray has received a
copy of a letter for the Deputy Minister of Munitions
. . .* began a cable from Zabotin to his Director, and
went on to quote a secret directive about war supplies.
*From Gray we have received materials on Torpex (high
explosive for depth bombs . . .)* said another cable.

Sometimes the Director in Moscow would ask Zabotin questions about Gray's reports. *In the mail of
23.8.44,* said one, *were received from you Gray's two
materials. . . . On the basis of the short and fragmentary data it is impossible to judge the methods and
work of the Canadian and English industry of war supplies . . .;* and the Director listed subjects on which
he wanted further details. Five days later, Zabotin told
Moscow that the task of obtaining those details would
be assigned to *Gray* and to two other spies.

But most of the information which *Gray* stole for Colonel Zabotin was far from "short and fragmentary." *We have received from Gray the whole correspondence on the question of the deformation of the shell in the channel of the barrel. Altogether 150 pages . . .* said one message to Moscow.

Besides being highly secret, much of *Gray's* material was highly technical as well. *The gun being slightly elevated, some liquid RDX/TNT flowed back along the grooves into the chamber . . .* began one long report on a conference of the Ordnance Board about the trials of a new shell filling, which he carefully copied on to a page of his loose-leaf notebook for the Russians.

Gray maintained this supply of stolen information for three years. Towards the end of that time, it seemed likely that post-war staff reductions would eventually lose him his job in the civil service. Through Sokolov, Zabotin ordered him to do everything possible to keep his position where he had access to so many secrets. But at the same time he cabled to the Director for approval of an alternative plan to set *Gray* up with an office as a geological consultant. *The expenses for organizing the office are as follows,* he explained; *rent of premises, $600 a year; wages for one clerk, $1,200; payment to Gray as a director, $4,200 a year; altogether it will require $7,000 a year . . . I beg to get your decision.* Who was this spy for whom Zabotin was willing to spend so much money?

Gray was the Russian's code-name for a sturdy, brown-haired man, successful, self-assured and intelligent, who had been a prosperous geological engineer before the war and had joined the Government service in 1941. He was a graduate of McGill University, and, with his spectacles, pipe and affable expression, some people thought he still looked like a university don.

Until July 1944, he worked for a government-owned company making chemicals and explosives. Then he became chief of the Records Division of the Ammunition Production Branch of the Department of Munitions and Supply. He was born in 1905 to parents who came from Russia. He was a secret communist, knew Carr and was friendly with several of Zabotin's other study-group spies. His name was Harold Samuel Gerson.

★   ★   ★

Among Gerson's communist associates was his wife's sister's husband, James Scotland Benning, a tall, round-faced man with dark hair, rimless spectacles and a thin, clipped moustache. Benning became interested in communist politics during the 1930's as a result, he said, of reading. Though he was never able to get through Marx's *Das Kapital* and found most of the other communist classics "too cumbersome," he was deeply impressed by a book by the Indian leader of the British Communist Party, Palme Dutt, "I was," he afterwards explained, "what you would call parlor pink, I believe, or what some of the more orthodox would call an arm-chair Bolshevik." His views led him into a number of communist-controlled "front" organizations: China Relief, the Civil Liberties League, the League against Fascism and War. For them, he did a good deal of voluntary work, "stuffing envelopes and things of that nature," he said. It was in those days that he got to know many of the people who later became spies for Colonel Zabotin: among them, Fred Rose.

During the war, Harold Gerson recommended him for a Government job. As a result, he joined the Department of Munitions and Supply in July 1942. Fred

Rose then suggested that he would be useful to the Russians. In January 1943 he was recruited to the military spy-ring, with whom he kept in touch through Nicolai Zheveinov, the *Tass* correspondent.

The information which Benning stole was enormous in quantity and very varied. It included Canadian production programs for aircraft and for ships, batches of cables sent by the British Ministry of Supply, and minutes of secret meetings held in his department. One of his thefts caused Colonel Zabotin particular satisfaction. It was a 14-page record of a meeting of a technical committee. To his report to Moscow, Zabotin added the comment: *See who was Secretary of the Meeting.* According to the signature at the foot of the document, the Secretary was Harold S. Gerson, Benning's brother-in-law and fellow spy.

For three years Benning worked for the Russians and became one of Zabotin's most trusted and productive spies. In one single list of documents sent by Zabotin to Moscow, Benning was credited with having stolen no fewer than seventy separate items. Meanwhile, his conscientious work in the Department of Munitions and Supply earned him an excellent reputation with his colleagues there. Seven months after he had started spying, his chief wrote to the head of the Personnel Branch of the Department: "He has a keen grasp of his duties and is doing an excellent job." Benning was promoted.

★   ★   ★

The motives which turned Gerson and Benning into Soviet spies are relatively simple. They were secret communists who had been gradually conditioned by their party until they found it natural to betray and steal and lie. The case of the next important spy to

join the military spy-ring before Zabotin's arrival was
a little different. He was Dr. Raymond Boyer, a scientist with an international reputation, a brilliant chem-
ist and a wealthy man. According to the Colonel's
records, he joined the ring early in 1943.

Boyer was a French-Canadian who was born to prosperous parents in Montreal. He graduated from McGill
University in 1930, and took his doctorate in chemistry
five years later. Then he studied at Harvard, Vienna
and Paris and returned to Canada in February 1937.
He was sufficiently rich to take no job. In 1938 he
joined a communist study-group in Montreal.

In the autumn of 1939, Dr. Boyer offered his services to the Canadian Government. He suggested that
he should be sent to Russia to find out the attitude of
the Soviet leaders towards the war. He seemed to have
no particular qualifications for such a mission and his
offer was politely turned down. But his scientific qualifications were well known. In July 1940, he joined the
National Research Council, a Canadian Government
organization which directed scientific war work, and
went to Toronto University to carry out research on
high explosives. He worked without a salary and paid
his own expenses. In September he moved to McGill
University at Montreal. There he was jointly in charge
of a project for developing a new process for making
a secret high explosive called RDX. This project was
successful. In June 1941, a pilot plant for making RDX
was built at Shawinigan Falls. That autumn a second
plant was built nearby, and in the spring of 1942 full-
scale production of RDX began. But Dr. Boyer's research work on the project continued until 1945.

Meanwhile, early in 1943, Dr. Boyer received a telephone call from Fred Rose, whom he had known since
1938. Rose invited him to visit his apartment. There

he told the scientist that the Russians wanted information about RDX. While Rose took notes, Boyer began to give him a description of the new process for making the explosive, and an account of the various ways in which it could be used. He completed his story at a series of later meetings, before each of which Rose would again telephone and invite Boyer to his home. Rose passed the information on to one of Zabotin's staff, and the Colonel then cabled it to Moscow. In this way the Russians learned enough about RDX to enable competent chemists to design a plant and produce the secret explosive in quantity. They also learned from Dr. Boyer, perhaps for the first time, that the Americans were carrying out experiments to use uranium for making an atomic bomb.

Afterward, Dr. Boyer explained that it was his "communist leaning" which made him betray these secrets to the Russians through Fred Rose. But he claimed that there was also another reason for his treachery. He said: "I felt throughout the work that it was unfortunate . . . that there was not closer scientific liaison in connection with such information between the Russian war effort and ours." And he added: "I still felt that it was of tremendous importance that there should be a full exchange of information between Russia and Canada and the United States and England." But like another scientist, an even more famous spy for Colonel Zabotin, he never explained how it could further the "full exchange of information" to help a spy-ring to steal official secrets from an ally for a government which never showed the slightest willingness to share its own secrets with any other country. As a scientist, Boyer was entitled to have views on the problem of exchanging scientific information. But only a communist scientist could have attempted to solve the problem in the way he chose.

★　　　　　★　　　　　★

With Rose and Carr as advisers and contact-men, and with well-placed spies like Willsher, Gerson, Benning and Boyer already working, Colonel Zabotin now set about the task of expanding his military spy-ring. More secret communists were recruited as spies, in the services and in other government departments. Some had access to technical information: top-secret research on fuses, explosives, radar and asdic. Others stole political secrets. One spy was a cipher clerk in the Department of External Affairs who gave Sokolov copies of diplomatic cables. Much of the technical information concerned post-war defense; not only the defense of Canada but of Britain and the United States as well. Part of the political information dealt with relations between Canada and the other Western Powers. For though Zabotin was mainly concerned with local Canadian secrets, his office was part of a big international network with interests—and spy-rings—in every country of the world.

Colonel Zabotin himself was involved in the international ramifications of the Russian Military Intelligence in more ways than one. Sometimes, for example, he was asked to cooperate in transferring spies from one country to another. Those arrangements were always made through Moscow, and were worked out in the greatest detail. Typical of them was a plan which Zabotin cabled to his Director at the end of April 1944, for the recognition and endorsement in London of a Canadian communist named Samuel Sol Burman.

In civil life, Burman was an insurance agent living in Montreal. He knew Fred Rose, and according to

Zabotin's records, he had joined the Communist Party in 1938, and had worked as an organizer during the time when the party was illegal. His wife had joined the party in 1939. He had a brother known as Ben. In April 1943, Burman enlisted into the Canadian army. He was trained to work on the Civil Affairs staff in occupied countries, and he was due to be sent to England in 1944.

Zabotin's message began: *I am communicating to you the arrangements for Burman's meeting in London. The meeting will take place two weeks after Burman's departure . . . at 15 o'clock on Sunday in front of the office of the High Commissioner for Canada, London, S.W. 1 (Canada House, Trafalgar Square) . . . Burman will be in civilian clothes—brown suit (tweed) checkered, without a hat, with a newspaper in his right hand. Pass-word "How's Elsie?" Burman will reply, "She's fine." Thereupon our man will hand to him a letter signed "Frank."*

Zabotin went on to explain that if the meeting at Trafalgar Square should fail, Burman would write to his wife giving the address of his London billet. She would then pass the address to Fred Rose, who would give it to one of Zabotin's staff. Zabotin would inform Moscow. If Moscow could arrange for their London man to meet Burman there, Rose would be told and Burman's wife would write him a letter including the sentence: *Ben has not been feeling too well.* Burman would then wait for the contact-man to find him at his billet. Meanwhile Zabotin sent a photograph of Burman and the letter signed *Frank* (which was from Rose) with a member of the Embassy staff to Moscow. It was not the Colonel's fault that, for unknown reasons, the meeting outside Canada House apparently never took place.

*   *   *

At about the same time that he was making these arrangements for Samuel Burman, Zabotin became involved in another, more complicated international transaction. It was in this way that he first heard of a stout, middle-aged Lithuanian woman called Germina Rabinowitch.

Germina Rabinowitch was born in Kaunas. She was educated in Moscow, Paris, Geneva and Heidelberg, was a doctor of economics and social science, and spoke Russian, English, French, German and Italian. With these qualifications she joined the International Labor Office in Geneva in 1929. In September 1940, the office was moved from Geneva to Montreal, and Germina Rabinowitch came over to Canada with other members of the staff. She lived at 539 Pine Avenue West in Montreal and, as an international employee, she carried a Canadian diplomatic card.

In December 1943, Germina Rabinowitch received a letter. It came from Geneva in the official bag. It was signed *Rachel,* and it read:

We live in the former apartment and we are working as previously in the old firm. Some two weeks ago Sisi sent you a telegram. Tell us how did your journey to Gisel's parents turn out. My health is excellent. Albert is sick and will probably leave his profession for a long time, he is laid up in bed. Relations with Lucy are good and she is a very good woman. Gisel's family is for some reason no longer interested in her, although up to this time there was support. Lucy's situation has improved. Sisi's position is sad. Please inform Gisel's parents that they must remit 6,700 dollars. This sum must be handed over through you. There are no other possi-

bilities. The Gisels must bear these expenses. Advise me about Aleksander where is he.

The writer of this letter was Rachel Dübendorfer: a member of a Soviet spy-ring operating against Germany from Switzerland, who was known to the Russians as *Sisi*. In a ready-made and obvious code, *Sisi's* letter told the story of how part of her spy-ring had been uncovered some months before by the Swiss police; how a leader, *Albert,* was in jail, and how the remaining members of the ring had lost contact with *Gisel's family,* that is with Moscow, and had run out of funds. She therefore asked Germina Rabinowitch to make contact with the Russians in Canada and to arrange with them to send money.

Germina Rabinowitch at once telephoned to the Soviet Embassy at Ottawa and asked for an appointment with the Counsellor, Tounkin. At first he refused to see her. She insisted and he finally agreed. But the interview was short and unsatisfactory. The Counsellor claimed to know nothing about the matter, and Germina Rabinowitch went back to Montreal empty-handed. She wrote to Rachel Dübendorfer that she had failed, and followed her letter with a cable on January 23rd. Hearing nothing more from the Russians, she wrote to Tounkin on March 9th, enclosing the text of Rachel Dübendorfer's first letter. There was no answer.

Then a second letter arrived from Geneva. *I have received your telegram,* it said. *Please inform Gisel's family that she should advise Znamensky 19 that Sisi is alive and works with Lucy. Lucy wanted to change the personnel but funds ran out. Albert is sick and is not interested in business. For the work of Sisi, Gisel's family must transfer 10,000 dollars. The transfer must be made by Germina personally through NY. . . . R.D.*

This was a dangerously obvious message, for Znamensky 19 is the address of the headquarters of the Russian Military Intelligence in Moscow. Germina Rabinowitch again telephoned the Russian Embassy. She also wrote Tounkin another letter enclosing the text of Rachel Dübendorfer's second message. It had taken four and a half months of persistent effort for Germina Rabinowitch to make contact with his military spyring.

The reason for this strange delay was the secrecy and rivalry which existed between the various Russian spy organizations in the Ottawa Embassy. Tounkin himself was probably quite honest when he told Germina Rabinowitch at the first interview that he knew nothing about *Sisi, Albert* and *Gisel*. Perhaps he suspected that she was a police agent or a provocateur. Only when her letter arrived, with the text of *Sisi's* message, did he mention the case to Pavlov, the representative of the N.K.V.D. Pavlov cabled to Moscow for instructions. He was told that this was a military espionage matter, and that he must take no action. He therefore said nothing to Zabotin, until *Sisi's* second message reached him about Znamensky 19. Two days later, on April 17th, Pavlov handed the papers to Zabotin's assistant, Lieutenant-Colonel Motinov. A telephone call was at once put through to Montreal. Germina Rabinowitch was told that in two weeks' time someone would visit her, and that meanwhile she must avoid all further contact with the Soviet Embassy. Then Zabotin sent in a full report to Moscow. The case worried him. "The copy of the second letter, which deals with Znamensky 19, was particularly prejudicial," commented Lieutenant-Colonel Motinov.

Two weeks later, on May 5th, 1944, Sergei Koudriavtzev visited Germina Rabinowitch in her office
in Montreal. He showed her a typewritten letter. *Dear
Germina*, it read. *Thank you very much indeed for your
care in our affairs and we hope that you will help us
in future. It is important for us to send a letter to Geneva . . . All expenses will be paid . . . Please wire
to Rachel or Alexander that Gisel's parents are interested about the health of Sisi and Paul and that they
will help them. We ask you to forward $10,000 . . .
Make arrangements with our representative about for-
warding of this sum of money to you in U.S.A. All your
personal expenses will be paid. With best regards,
Gisel.*

On May 20th, Germina Rabinowitch visited New
York, on a business trip for the International Labor
Office. There, at a hotel, she was handed 10,000 dollars
by a representative of the Russian Military Intelligence.
She took this money to a contact, who conducted a
Watch Company from his midtown New York office.
By placing the fund in his hands, she arranged its
transfer to Geneva. On her return to Canada, Germina
Rabinowitch had three more meetings with Koudriavtzev, on street corners at Montreal. At the third of
these, on August 28th, she was able to tell him that she
had heard from her contact, who had received a cable
from Geneva which read *Thanks for the warm greetings*. At last Russian money had reached the Swiss spy-
ring.

Meanwhile, having found Germina Rabinowitch so
reliable in these financial transactions, Colonel Zabotin
had decided that she might also be useful as a local
spy. At her last meeting with Koudriavtzev she brought
him a report on the organization and personalities of
the International Labor Office where she worked. With

it was a covering note: "I am, of course, at your disposal for any supplementary information . . ."

*   *   *

The reasons which brought Germina Rabinowitch into the Soviet military spy-ring are still not entirely clear. Afterward she herself gave an explanation. She had last seen her parents in Lithuania some years before. They were very old and suffering great hardships, and she wanted to help them to migrate to the United States. "I had perhaps the foolish idea," she said, "that with rendering service . . . to Rachel, I might have some kind of possibilities in helping my parents, who were in very great danger there in Lithuania." But in fact her parents died in Lithuania, having been refused permission to leave by the Russians. "I did not get anything from them, because the small service I asked for they did not render it to me, even when I asked for my parents," was her final disillusioned comment.

VIII

Medals for Grant

★

By March of 1945, Colonel Zabotin already had good reason to be pleased. His long, daily cipher telegrams to his Director, and the heavy diplomatic bags which followed them to Moscow, proved that his spy-ring had become a major source of military and political secrets stolen from Canada and the Western Powers. But the next six months were to bring still more spectacular results. Between March and August of 1945, Colonel Zabotin reached the peak of his success.

Early in March, an anonymous note arrived on the Editor's desk in the office of the military magazine *Canadian Affairs*. The magazine was published by the Information to Armed Forces section of the Wartime Information Board. Its offices were at 139½ Sparks Street, Ottawa. The note asked the Editor to meet an unnamed person at the corner of Rideau Street. A few days later, the Editor kept the appointment. There he found a Russian. After a few minutes' conversation, the Russian handed him a typewritten paper. This paper has been preserved in the official report of the Royal Canadian Commission (Ottawa). It read:

1. *The scheme of your group will be approximately such as it is shown below.*

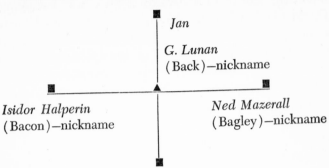

Jan

G. Lunan
(Back)—nickname

Isidor Halperin
(Bacon)—nickname

Ned Mazerall
(Bagley)—nickname

Dornforth Smith
(Badeau)—nickname
You will only know me (as Jan) but nobody else

2. *What we would like you to do:*
   (a) *To characterize the scales and works carrying out at National Research and also the scheme of this Department.*
   (b) *To conduct the work of "Bacon," "Badeau" and "Bagley." It is advisable to put the following tasks to them separately. . . .*

There followed a list of wanted information. Then:
All the materials and documents to be passed by Bagley, Bacon and Badeau to be signed by their nicknames as stated above.

If your group have the documents which you will not be able to give us irrevocably, we shall photograph them and return back to you. I beg you to instruct every man separately about conspiracy in our work. . . .

At the end were the words *P.S. After studying burn it*. When he had read this paper, the Editor agreed to see the Russian again on March 28th.

This meeting on the corner of Rideau Street was the

beginning of Colonel Zabotin's 'B Group' of spies. *Jan,* the Russian in charge, was Lieutenant-Colonel Rogov. *Back,* the Editor of *Canadian Affairs,* was Lieutenant David Gordon Lunan. The note which arrived on his desk was not unexpected. According to Zabotin's records, Lunan was a member of the Communist Party. He was also a member of the communist-dominated Quebec Committee for Allied Victory, and he had known Fred Rose for at least two years. It was Rose who, some days before, had met Lunan on a train and sounded him about working as a Soviet spy.

Lunan was a tall, thin-faced Scotsman from Kirkcaldy, 31 years old. He had come to Canada in 1938 and had worked for advertising agencies in Montreal until January 1943, when he had enlisted in the Canadian Army. He had been commissioned three months later, and in the next year had been assigned to the Wartime Information Board and put in charge of *Canadian Affairs.* In his work there, he had no technical knowledge or access to secret information likely to interest the Russians. But as a contact-man he was well placed.

Of the three spies of whom Rogov had told him to take charge (his note had garbled some of the names), Durnford Smith and Edward Wilfred Mazerall were engaged on secret work for the National Research Council, and Israel Halperin was a Major in the Department of National Defense. Of the three, only Durnford Smith was known to Lunan, but they all knew Fred Rose, who first suggested them to the Russians.

Lunan at once set out to organize his group. He began with Durnford Smith, a research engineer in the micro-wave section of the Radio Branch of the National Research Council. Like several of the other spies, he was a graduate of McGill University. He was born of Canadian parents in 1912, and for five years before joining the Council, he had worked for the Bell Telephone Company in Montreal.

Although Lunan knew Durnford Smith and had every reason to think he would cooperate, he broached the subject of spying cautiously. He did not want to uncover himself too completely at first, and Smith was equally careful. After some rather veiled conversation —"We were fencing with words, as it were," Lunan afterwards explained—Smith said that he would think it over. He then checked up independently on Lunan, probably with Rose. At the next meeting with Lunan, he accepted. He later became much the most cooperative of Lunan's three spies. His own job was chiefly secret research on radio-location, radar and other navigational aids. But he had contact with other sections of the National Research Council. And he had access to the Council's library of secret technical documents.

The second member of Lunan's group was Major Israel Halperin, a Canadian of Russian parents, a professor of mathematics at Queen's University at Kingston, who had joined the army in 1942. At this time Halperin was in the Directorate of Artillery, where he worked on a number of secret projects, had access to all secret documents concerning weapons and explosives and knew about all new discoveries which were made available to the Artillery. Lunan telephoned to Halperin in mid-March and took him out to lunch. He explained his proposal in much the same language he had used with Smith. Halperin agreed, but at first his attitude rather disconcerted Lunan. He took the line that most so-called secret work was a joke, and he did not seem to understand the seriousness of what Lunan was suggesting. But he left Lunan with the impression that he was keen and would be helpful.

On March 28th Lunan met Rogov again and handed

him a long report which he had typed out in his office. *Dear Mother and Father,* it began, *General approach to work: Your written instructions are understood and some preliminary work has been accomplished on the specific tasks set.* He then went on to report that he had made contact with Smith and Halperin, but had so far been unable to see Mazerall. *I shall take things slow with him for a start,* he wrote. *I plan to develop his acquaintance as much as possible and give him confidence by collaborating on some scientific articles.*

It was not until June that Lunan eventually managed to recruit Mazerall to his group. He telephoned to him at his office, took him to lunch at the cafeteria of the Château Laurier, and then for a drive in his car. He began the conversation by asking Mazerall's advice on the circuit for a radio-phonograph that he was building. Then he gradually led the conversation round to scientific secrets. At a second meeting a few days later, Lunan explained more clearly what he wanted. Mazerall agreed, and Lunan gave him a slip of paper on which Rogov had listed a series of technical questions to which he wanted answers. In this way Mazerall began his spy work. At twenty-nine, he was the youngest member of the "B Group," a tall, broad-shouldered man, with a shock of untidy hair. He was an electrical engineer and had been employed by the Canadian Broadcasting Corporation before he joined the Research Council in 1942 to do work on radar. He knew several of Zabotin's other spies and, like Kathleen Willsher, had been a member of Agatha Chapman's study-group in Ottawa. His wife was a well-known pianist.

Meanwhile, Lunan had been meeting Rogov at regular intervals since March, passing on written reports based on information supplied by the other two spies and receiving new instructions from the Russian. Occasionally he supplied material himself, but always on general, non-technical subjects. In May, for example, Rogov asked him to write a report on the elections to the Federal Parliament and the pre-election campaign, describing the role and significance of each party. This Lunan duly did.

At his meetings with Lunan, Rogov often handed over money for distribution among the group. These sums he noted in the files after each meeting. On April 4th, for example, he made an entry showing that he had paid Lunan 190 dollars: 100 for Lunan himself and 30 each for the other three spies.

Soon afterwards, Lunan began to have trouble with Major Halperin, who was apparently particularly upset when Lunan, on instructions from Rogov, asked him to try to steal some samples of uranium for the Russians. In his third report to Rogov dated July 5th, Lunan wrote: *I spent a whole evening with Bacon with most disappointing results . . . I shall continue to see him but he gave me definitely no encouragement last time.* In another report Lunan added: *I think that at present he had a further understanding of the essence of my requests and he has a particular dislike for them.* A little later Rogov noted in his records: *Bacon—categorically refused to give any kind of written information and also documents to be photographed. A possibility exists, but he is afraid.* But by word of mouth Halperin had already passed some important stolen secrets. He had described in detail plans to set up a new Canadian Army research establishment dealing with explosives, and he had given details of a secret electronic shell.

Lunan's disappointment with Halperin, however, was amply compensated by the eagerness of Durnford Smith, who had already provided a great deal of information. But much of this information was highly technical, and Lunan, who was a writer but not a scientist, could not understand it. Rogov discussed the problem with Colonel Motinov. They decided that Smith was sufficiently valuable to them to justify taking an extra risk. *In the future for the purpose of more efficient direction,* Motinov noted in the file, *it is expedient to detach him from Back's group and to key him up as an independent contact.* So Rogov asked Lunan to arrange a direct meeting.

On July 5th, Lunan met Smith near the Laurier Bridge on the Driveway in Ottawa. Together they walked round to a street corner, where Rogov picked them up in a Soviet Embassy car. Smith got into the back with the Russian while Lunan sat in front next to the driver. For forty minutes they drove round while Rogov talked confidentially to Smith.

Makes a good impression, Rogov noted afterwards in the file. *At the meeting behaved very cautiously, somewhat cowardly. Brought material for photographing on radio-locators.* A little farther down was the entry: *Handed out 100 dollars; he took the money readily.* At that meeting, Rogov also gave Smith a series of detailed questions about a new 750-million candle-power flash bomb and about aerial photographic apparatus. Next day, he sent him a further assignment on secret radio devices.

Soon Smith was producing immense quantities of information. On August 27th Zabotin cabled to his Director: *We have received from Badeau 17 top secret and secret documents (English, American and Canadian) on the question of magnicoustics, radio-locators for field artillery: three secret scientific-research journals of the year 1945. Altogether about 700 pages. In the course of the day we were able to photograph all the documents. . . . And he added: I consider it es-sential to examine the whole library of the Scientific Research Council.* The photographing of the documents was carried out under the supervision of Captain Gorshkov, Zabotin's "driver," in the well-equipped photographic laboratory in the Military Attaché's house at Range Road. The library of the National Research Council was a collection of highly secret papers which only selected officials were supposed to see.

★   ★   ★

All this information was very welcome to Colonel Zabotin. Despite the difficulties with the cautious Major Halperin, Lunan's "B Group" was working well. But now one subject began to interest the Russians above all others. It became Zabotin's chief target during 1945. That subject was the atom bomb.

By the spring of 1945, work on this most secret project was nearing its climax. That summer, on July 16th, the first perfected bomb was to be exploded in the Alamogordo Desert in New Mexico. Twenty-one days later the Japanese city of Hiroshima was annihilated by another atom bomb. Meanwhile, Zabotin had already sent to Moscow some scraps of information on this subject. From Boyer he had learnt of a uranium plant under construction, and had cabled to his Director: *As a result of experiments carried out with uranium, it has been found that uranium may be used for filling bombs, which is already in fact being done.* Durnford Smith had reported that the most secret work he knew of was on nuclear physics—the bombardment of radio-active substances to produce energy—and that this was "more hush-hush than radar." In April, Smith had suggested that he should try to have himself transferred to this work, but Colonel Motinov had turned the suggestion down. In July, Halperin had told Lunan that he was *curious about the Chalk River Plant and the manufacture of Uranium. He claims that there is a great deal of talk and speculation on the subject but that nothing is known outside of the small and carefully guarded group completely in the know.* It was to this small and carefully guarded group that the Russians turned their attention.

★   ★   ★

British scientists working on atomic energy were first put under a central government directorate in October 1941. At the end of 1942 they began to exchange information with government scientists in the United States. Early in 1943, for reasons of safety, most of the work was transferred from England to Canada: to laboratories in Montreal and to an experimental plant—a heavy-water pile—at Chalk River, Ontario. In July 1944, Sir John Cockcroft, Jacksonian Professor of Natural Philosophy at Cambridge and later head of Harwell, the British center for atomic research, was made director of the project.

A senior member of his team in Montreal was an able young physicist, a lecturer from London University, who had joined the atomic energy project in England in April 1942, and had come over to Canada nine months later. He was a quiet, unobtrusive-looking little man, shy and rather lonely. He had a bulging forehead, thin brown hair, and small, weak eyes. He lived in his own flat in Swaile Avenue, Montreal. His work was more concerned with the wider aspects of atomic research than with the atom bomb itself. Certainly, he did not know how to make the bomb; no one in Canada had that knowledge. But he did know about the work in his own laboratory, about the production of plutonium, about the heavy-water pile at Chalk River, and about the graphite piles in the state of Washington. He also knew more than any other British scientist about American atomic research at Argonne Laboratory in Chicago which he had visited three times in 1944. He was, in fact, in possession of immensely secret and immensely valuable information. He was also a Soviet spy.

Russian Military Intelligence had already made contact with this man while he was still in England. When and how they did so is still a mystery. He was not a known Communist Party member although, since his undergraduate days at Cambridge in the early 'thirties, he had made no secret of his so-called "left-wing" views. In September, 1936, he had gone to Leningrad as a tourist, and soon after his return from Russia he joined the editorial board of the *Scientific Worker*, the journal of the National Association of Scientific Workers in which many communists were active. Later, in Canada, he also joined the newly formed Canadian Association of Scientific Workers which was likewise communist-penetrated and of which Dr. Boyer was the National President. But to his colleagues he always seemed almost entirely preoccupied with his scientific work. To the Russians he was known by the code-name *Alek*.

Early in 1945, Colonel Zabotin was ordered by his Director to make contact with this man. It was suggested that he should do so through Fred Rose. But the Colonel thought it wiser not to use a well-known communist in so delicate and dangerous a job. He asked permission to use one of his own staff instead. Moscow agreed. Lieutenant Pavel Angelov was given the assignment. He located the scientist easily, by looking up his home address in the Montreal telephone book. Then he went to Montreal. It was evening when he arrived at the flat at Swaile Avenue, and the scientist himself opened the door. After a few words, Angelov suddenly said, confidentially but distinctly, "*How's Michael?*" The scientist's manner abruptly changed. He had recognized the Soviet password.

Angelov later told his colleagues in the Military Attaché's Department that at that first interview the scientist had acted as though he had been "trapped." But he did agree to spy. And he accepted 200 dollars which Angelov had hidden in an empty whisky bottle, together with a second whisky bottle which was full. This meeting took place on April 12th. It was followed by a series of further meetings with Angelov, at one of which *Alek* was paid a further 500 dollars.

In July, the scientist heard that he was to be sent back to England. He told Angelov, and Colonel Zabotin duly cabled the news to Moscow. On July 28th, twelve days after the first secret atomic bomb exploded in the Alamogordo Desert, his Director replied with this instruction: *Try to get from him before departure information on the progress of uranium.* On August 9th, three days after the Hiroshima bomb, Zabotin answered with the most important message of his career:

To the Director.

Facts given by Alek. (1) *The test of the atomic bomb was conducted in New Mexico (with "49," "94-239"). The bomb dropped on Japan was made of uranium 235. . . .*

(2) *Alek handed over to us a platinum with 162 micrograms of uranium 233 in the form of oxide in a thin lamina. . . .*

Grant.

Actually, the scientist had given the Russians a long written report and two stolen samples of uranium. One was in a small glass tube, a slightly enriched specimen of U.235. The other was a very thin deposit of U.233 on a platinum foil, wrapped in a piece of paper. Colonel Zabotin thought these samples of such importance that he ordered Lieutenant-Colonel Motinov to fly at once to Moscow and deliver them personally to Military Intelligence headquarters. A few days later, by a curious coincidence, Colonel Zabotin himself was invited to a fishing trip by a Canadian who lived near the Chalk River experimental plant. From a motor-boat, he was able to see and photograph the outside of the building.

★   ★   ★

Apart from his reports on atomic energy the English scientist had also given information on other subjects. Once he reported on a junior colleague, an Englishman working in his laboratory in Montreal, whom the Russians were thinking of recruiting to the spy-ring. He advised them not to do so and Moscow eventually turned the scheme down. Another report was a description of an American electronic shell. But the time for his departure was now drawing near. On Moscow's orders Zabotin prepared a scheme for him to make fresh contact with Soviet Military Intelligence when he reached London. The Director consulted his representatives in London and cabled to Ottawa a new version of the Colonel's plan.

In great detail, he set out the arrangements for the meeting. At eight o'clock on an agreed evening, *Alek* was to walk from the Tottenham Court Road along the south side of Great Russell Street, carrying under his left arm a copy of *The Times*. The contact-man was to walk along the same street from the opposite direction holding a copy of *Picture Post* in his left hand. They were to meet in front of the British Museum near the corner of Museum Street, and the contact-man was to ask *Alek*: "What is the shortest way to the Strand?" *Alek* was to answer: "Well, come along. I am going that way." Then, before starting to talk business, *Alek* would give the password "Best regards from Michael."

Soon afterward the scientist left Canada for England. He moved into rooms at Stafford Terrace, off Kensington High Street in London, and took up work as senior reader in Physics at King's College in the Strand. But neither he nor his contact-man kept the appointment outside the British Museum. By that time *Alek*, better known as Dr. Allan Nunn May, was under observation by the police.

★   ★   ★

At the end of August, however, Colonel Zabotin was untroubled by any warnings of the future. On the contrary, he was highly pleased. A cable of congratulation had just reached him from his Director, announcing that he had been awarded two decorations in recognition of his work: the Order of the Red Banner and the Order of the Red Star. The Director added: *I wish you further success in your honorable work.* This news greatly cheered the Colonel who, like other Soviet officials—and particularly officials working abroad—lived in a state of constant apprehension about his standing with his superiors in Moscow. "Now I can go back without any worries," he confided to one of his colleagues. A few days later he renewed an application for home leave. His son Vladimir had just finished his education and the Colonel was anxious to arrange his entry into the Moscow Artillery School from which he himself had graduated in 1924. He sent a personal cable to his Director's chief, Colonel-General Kouznetzov, and asked if he might now visit Moscow.

The disaster happened six days later.

IX

The Missing Lieutenant

★

It was not until the early afternoon of September 6th, 1945, that the staff of the Military Attaché's department realized that something was wrong. The Colonel's cipher officer, who was due on duty at midday, was not in his office in Room 12. The steel safe had been locked the night before and the sealed cable bag was in its place, but when they were opened, some files and papers were gone from the safe and cables from the bags. There was not a great number missing; but in that office every single document was of the utmost secrecy, and extraordinary precautions were always taken to keep them safe. A thorough search in Room 12 failed to find them.

Meanwhile there had been no message from the cipher officer, Gouzenko. The security guard behind the two sealed doors in the secret wing said that he had checked out normally at about eight the previous evening. The Embassy doorman remembered seeing him leave the building a few moments later. During the afternoon, when there was still no word from the cipher officer, Lieutenant Lavrentiev of the Military Attaché's staff was sent out to find him.

At this stage, there was no possible reason for suspecting Lieutenant Gouzenko. Like all the other officers of Colonel Zabotin's department, he had been selected and trained with the utmost care. He had done well at

school and at 17 he had joined the Young Communist
League. He had been accepted by the Academy of En-
gineering, and, after two months there, had been transferred to an army intelligence training center. He had
then served for a year at the Military Intelligence headquarters in Moscow. Before coming to Canada with
Colonel Zabotin in 1943, he had been under routine
investigation for five months by the N.K.V.D. They had
pronounced him reliable in every way. In his work in
Ottawa, he had been conscientious and efficient. He was
now preparing to return to Russia and, like other Soviet
officials going home, had been laying in a store of
canned food and clothing to take with him. His superiors thought well of him, and his relations with his
colleagues had been good.

With a companion from the Embassy, Lieutenant
Lavrentiev went round to 511 Somerset Street where
Gouzeko had his flat. Both men were in civilian clothes.
For some time they kept the front of the building under
observation from a bench in the park on to which it
faced. Then, at about half-past six, Lavrentiev walked
into the building, up the stairs to flat number 4 and
called out "Open the door!" There was no reply. But
Lavrentiev heard the sound of a small child running
across the floor. Puzzled, he went back to the Embassy
and reported what had happened to Colonel Zabotin.
The Colonel reluctantly decided to call in the N.K.V.D.
He was not on particularly good terms with Pavlov, the
head of the Embassy's secret police department, with
whom he had been involved in inter-departmental quarrels in the past. He had once complained of the "hooli-
gan" methods of Pavlov's staff. But this was clearly the
N.K.V.D.'s affair. He found Pavlov and explained the
situation. There was some discussion, and then Pavlov
called for an Embassy car. With Lieutenant-Colonel

Rogov and Lieutenant Angelov of Zabotin's staff, and his own cipher officer Farafotnov, he drove round to Somerset Street. The party arrived at Gouzenko's flat at 11:30. Pavlov knocked, but again there was no reply. Then the door of the next flat opened and its owner, a Canadian Air Force sergeant, looked out. Pavlov asked him where Gouzenko was. "You got me, buddy," replied the sergeant and shut his door. The Russians had a short discussion in the hall. They walked downstairs. Then they suddenly came back, knocked softly at Gouzenko's door again and broke it down.

A few moments later, two police constables arrived. They found all the lights on in flat 4 and the Russians busily ransacking it. Pavlov was inside a clothes cupboard and Lieutenant-Colonel Rogov in another. The police asked what was going on. Pavlov answered that the owner of the flat was in Toronto and that they had his permission to collect some Embassy papers from it. When one of the policemen commented that it was curious that they had had to break the door down, Pavlov answered that the flat was Russian property and that they could do what they liked there. Rogov then complained that the policemen had insulted them, and Pavlov ordered them to leave. The police asked them for their identity documents and, when they saw their diplomatic cards, sent for an Inspector. Inspector Macdonald arrived some minutes later. He sized up the situation and asked the Russians to wait while he went to make a few inquiries. While he was gone, they left.

Back at the Embassy, another anxious conference was held. Gouzenko's disappearance now looked extremely sinister: at all costs he must be caught. It was decided to accuse him of stealing money and to ask the Canadian Government to find him. Next day a diplomatic note was sent to the Department of External Affairs.

The Embassy of the U.S.S.R. asks the Department of External Affairs to seek and arrest I. Gouzenko and to hand him over for deportation as a capital criminal, who has stolen money belonging to the Embassy, it said. And it added a strong complaint about "rude treatment" of Embassy officials by the police. When the Canadian Government asked for details about the stolen money, the Embassy gave no answer. It reported Gouzenko's disappearance to Moscow and, a few days later, it sent a second note to the Department of External Affairs.

Confirming its communication in the note No. 35 of September 7th of the fact that Gouzenko had robbed public funds, the Embassy, upon instructions from the Government of the U.S.S.R. repeats its request to the Government of Canada to apprehend Gouzenko and his wife, and without trial, to hand them over to the Embassy for deportation to the Soviet Union.

The Soviet Government expresses the hope that the Government of Canada will fulfil its request.

The request was not fulfilled. For the next three months Colonel Zabotin and his colleagues were completely in the dark. There was no further sign of Gouzenko and the missing papers. His whereabouts and his motive for disappearing remained a mystery. The affair was not reported in the press and the Canadian Government made no further reference to it. And there were no apparent repercussions on the spy-ring. None of Zabotin's Canadian spies seemed to have been affected. There were no arrests and none of them reported anything suspicious.

What explanation Colonel Zabotin gave to his Director in Moscow of the events of September 6th will probably never be known by anyone outside Soviet Military Intelligence. The disaster must have seemed all the greater to him coming, as it did, so soon after a series of spectacular successes. But it is a little doubtful whether those successes helped him with his masters. He left Canada secretly in the first week of December and was last seen by two American customs men climbing the gangway of the Soviet ship *Alexander Suvorov* in New York harbor. That evening, without complying with regulations, the *Suvorov* sailed for the Soviet Union. Newspaper reports later announced that the hearty, healthy Colonel had died suddenly a few days after reaching Russia.

★   ★   ★

But though little is known about Colonel Zabotin after the first week of September 1945, except his departure and reported death, almost everything is now known about Gouzenko. His disappearance from the Embassy that evening was the culmination of a plan which had begun forming in his mind a year before.

He had been joined in Canada by his wife and small son soon after his arrival in June 1943, and the family had then set up house in the Somerset Street flat. They were happy in Ottawa, it seems, and the unexpected freedom and prosperity of Canadian life impressed them very deeply. This was not at all what they had been taught to expect of a "capitalist" country, and it was infinitely better than anything they had known in Russia. At the same time Gouzenko himself could not help comparing Canadian wartime generosity to the Soviet Union, with his own Government's double-faced response. While the Government of Canada was sending Russia great quantities of war supplies, and individual Canadians were collecting money for Russian welfare, Soviet officials, including himself, were busy building a fifth column of spies and traitors as though Canada were an enemy nation.

With thoughts like these already troubling him, Gouzenko learned in September 1944 that his Director had ordered his recall to Moscow. It was then that he first seriously considered the possibility of refusing to return. But the need for an immediate decision was removed when Colonel Zabotin successfully pleaded Gouzenko's usefulness in Ottawa and was allowed by the Director provisionally to keep him. He remained undisturbed in his work in the cipher office until the next June when a Lieutenant Koulakov arrived. This was Gouzenko's replacement. For the next few weeks they worked together until the new man was thoroughly familiar with the documents and routine. Then, in August, the Director again called for the return of Gouzenko and his family to Russia. This time there was no chance of postponement. Colonel Zabotin ordered him to prepare to sail on the next available Soviet ship. But by now Gouzenko had taken his decision. He started to make his final preparations.

Each time he found himself alone in his office, he ran through the files. He made a selection of the most secret and informative documents and turned down the corner of each so that he could locate it in a hurry. Whenever Zabotin or one of his other chiefs gave him scraps of paper for destruction in the incinerator in Room 14, he read them over carefully and, if they were of interest, quietly took them home. He hid them on a shelf in the kitchen of his flat and kept a matchbox close beside them.

On the evening of September 5th, Gouzenko stayed late at his office. He was alone in Room 12. Most of his colleagues, he knew, were at a film show, and he expected to be undisturbed. A few minutes before eight, he quickly took the marked files and papers from the safe, and a handful of cables from the cable box. These he hid inside his shirt. Then he locked the safe, sealed the bag, checked out and left the Embassy for the last time.

Most men in his position would have gone straight to the Canadian police and asked for their protection. But Gouzenko had seen too much of Soviet spy-work to do that. He was afraid that the police might have been penetrated by Pavlov's N.K.V.D. men who would denounce him and have him handed back to the Russians. He had no illusions about what would happen then; he was certain that he would be killed. He therefore went where he thought it least likely that there would be Russian spies: to the office of a leading daily newspaper. He hoped that press publicity for his story might protect him from his colleagues. But at the *Ottawa Journal* in Queen Street he was told firmly that the Editor was out. A harassed subordinate listened impatiently to him for a moment and then advised him to go to the police. The *Journal* had missed the biggest Canadian news story in a generation. It was fortunate that it had, though Gouzenko could not know it at the time. And time was running out.

Anxious and depressed, he went home to his flat and told his wife what had happened. Together they collected up all the secret papers—the scraps from the kitchen shelf and the documents he had brought away that evening—and hid them under the pillow. Then they went to bed and slept fitfully until early the next day. That morning Gouzenko no longer dared to leave his wife and child alone in the flat. He took them with him, with the documents in his wife's handbag. First they went back to the *Ottawa Journal* but were again told to go to the police. Then they tried the Ministry of Justice. The Minister's secretary told them that the Minister could not see them. Eventually, the secretary of the

Crown Attorney, impressed by their urgent pleading (Gouzenko's wife was by now in tears), succeeding in informing the Under-Secretary of State for External Affairs, who telephoned to the Prime Minister. The Prime Minister gave this instruction: "Tell the Russian to go back to the Russian Embassy with his papers."

Almost in despair, the Gouzenkos returned home. They went into the building by the back entrance. Then, peering cautiously from a front window, Gouzenko saw two men sitting on a park bench, looking up at the flat. They were in civilian clothes but he recognized one of them as Lieutenant Lavrentiev. A moment later Lavrentiev came up and knocked on the door.

Gouzenko decided that he and his family were now in immediate danger. He took them on to the balcony which was shared with two other flats and asked his neighbor, Sergeant Main, if he would look after the child if anything happened to him and his wife. He explained that they were expecting an attempt on their lives. At that moment Lavrentiev walked slowly down the lane behind the building, directly below them. This must have convinced the sergeant, for he agreed to take the child, and set off on a bicycle to call the police. Meanwhile, the Goukenzos' other neighbor, Mrs. Elliot from flat number 6, had come on to the balcony and invited the whole family to stay the night with her. They accepted gratefully. The police arrived soon afterwards in a prowl car and, after hearing Gouzenko's story, agreed to keep the house under observation for the night. They arranged that a bathroom light should be switched off as a signal if they were needed. Some time later, Pavlov and the other three Russians arrived at number 4. Gouzenko saw them through the keyhole of the door of number 6 and gave the signal. The police came up at once.

After the Russians had eventually left, Gouzenko and his family spent the rest of the night under police guard in Mrs. Elliot's flat. Early next morning, the morning of September 7th, they were taken for their protection to the Headquarters of the Royal Canadian Mounted Police. There, at last, Gouzenko told his story.

Now that he had found someone prepared to listen, it did not take him long to convince the Canadian authorities of the seriousness of what he had to tell. The Prime Minister was informed that he was in the hands of the police and a full, secret inquiry was immediately ordered. But the task of assembling and checking Gouzenko's story was by no means easy. He himself had never met a Canadian spy. His evidence consisted only of what he could remember from his office and of more than a hundred assorted documents which he had brought with him. They ranged from complete files to small scraps of paper torn from notebooks. There were dozens of reports handwritten in Russian by Zabotin, Motinov and Rogov. There was a cable file which he had been given weeks before to put in the incinerator and which was listed in the Colonel's books as burned. There were photographs and there were messages written by the spies themselves.

Gouzenko was moved to a special headquarters which was set up for the inquiry at Rockcliffe Barracks on the outskirts of Ottawa: a training depot for the Royal Canadian Mounted Police. It was well guarded and the inner buildings were surrounded by a high steel fence. Here Inspector Leopold took charge of the investigations.

It did not take long to confirm the authenticity of many of Gouzenko's papers. Experts discoverd that the handwriting of the Russian documents tallied with entries in a visitors' book belonging to hospitable Canadians who had entertained Colonel Zabotin and his two assistants. Four of Gouzenko's cables were found to be exact copies of secret telegrams received by the Department of External Affairs only a few weeks before. A list of code names was compiled and the real identities of the spies worked out. Gouzenko had selected his material with great skill. By September 21st, fifteen days after his disappearance, Commissioner Wood, Inspector Leopold's chief, was ready with a first report for the Canadian Prime Minister, Mackenzie King.

So serious were the implications of the Commissioner's report that a week later Mr. Mackenzie King himself flew to Washington with the Under-Secretary of State for External Affairs for a secret conference with President Truman. J. Edgar Hoover, head of the F.B.I., was called to the White House and ordered to keep in close touch with the Canadian police. Then the Canadian Prime Minister sailed for England. On October 6th he met Mr. Attlee, then Prime Minister, at Chequers. Sir Harold Scott, Commissioner of Scotland Yard, was sent for and told the facts. On his way back to Canada, Mr. Mackenzie King again called at Washington. Soon afterwards Mr. Attlee flew to America with his chief atomic energy advisers for a three-day conference with the President on the naval yacht *Sequoia* anchored in the Potomac River. He then went on to Ottawa for another meeting with Mr. Mackenzie King. But the purpose of all these meetings was kept a closely guarded secret.

★   ★   ★

During all this time, the members of the spy-ring who had been identified were under discreet police surveillance. Some of them were quietly moved, without arousing their suspicions, to new jobs where they no longer had access to secret information. On October 6th, 1945, a secret Order-in-Council was enacted which allowed the questioning and detention of the suspects without normal legal formalities. On February 5th another Order-in-Council set up a Royal Commission to investigate the communication by "public officials and other persons in positions of trust," of "secret and confidential information to agents of a foreign Power." On February 14th, the Prime Minister sent for the head of the Soviet Embassy. The Ambassador had left for Moscow a few days after Colonel Zabotin's departure, on what he described as a routine visit, though he never returned to Ottawa. Nikolai Belokhvostikov, the Chargé d'Affaires, came to the Prime Minister's office in his place. Mr. Mackenzie King informed him that, on the following day, he intended to make a grave announcement. Then he read him the text. It stated that there had been disclosures of secret information "to unauthorized persons including some members of the staff of a foreign mission to Canada." The Prime Minister explained that that foreign mission was the Soviet Embassy. Next day, the statement was published. It was the first official announcement of the discovery of the spy-ring.

On that same morning of February 15, 1946, the police made their first thirteen arrests. Not one of the arrested spies had any notion that, for five months, each of them had been under close and constant watch. The thirteen included Kathleen Willsher, Eric Adams, Harold Gerson, J. S. Benning, Dr. Boyer and Gordon Lunan and the three spies of his "B Group": Durnford Smith, Major Halperin and Edward Mazerall. On the same day, Commander Leonard Burt of the Special Branch spoke to Dr. Nunn May in London. A fortnight later, May too was arrested. The arrest of Fred Rose in his flat in Ottawa followed on March 15th. Meanwhile, Sam Carr, the expert in secret frontier crossings, had disappeared abroad. He was not caught until nearly three years later in New York.

The arrested spies were taken to Rockcliffe Barracks for interrogation. Then, in turn, they were called before the Royal Commission. The Commission had many advantages over an ordinary court of law. It could decide its own procedure and accept whatever evidence it thought was relevant. It was not concerned with punishment, for its only task was to find the facts. On the facts, its findings were legally as authoritative as those of the highest Law Court. It worked for five months, and its report was published on June 27, 1946.

In that report, Colonel Zabotin's spy-ring was described. It was, the Royal Commission said: *a malignant growth, the full penetration of which we did not know, but which was alive and expanding, working in secret below ground, directed against the safety and interests of Canada by a foreign power and made up of Canadian citizens who, while giving lip allegiance to this country and the oaths of allegiance and secrecy they had taken, were in truth and deed solely devoted to that foreign power, believing it to be the supreme exponent of ideas to which they had given themselves as much as if they were its citizens, and not citizens of this country.* In this summary of findings, the Commission added that membership in communist organizations or a sympathy towards communist ideologies was the "primary force" which caused the Canadian spies to act as they did.

Of those spies a few, like Kathleen Willsher and Doc-

tor Boyer, admitted their actions and motives with some
frankness to the Commission. Others were evasive.
Some, like Rose, refused to speak at all. In London,
Doctor Nunn May confessed his guilt and signed a brief
statement. *About a year ago, whilst in Canada, I was
contacted by an individual whose identity I refuse to
divulge . . . he sought information from me concerning atomic research. I gave and had given very careful
consideration to correctness of making sure that development of atomic energy was not confined to U.S.A.
I took the very painful decision that it was necessary to
convey general information on atomic energy and to
make sure that it was taken seriously. . . . The whole
affair was extremely painful to me and I only embarked
on it because I felt this was a contribution I could make
to the safety of mankind. I certainly did not do it for
gain.* His statement confirmed that he had stolen samples of U.233 and U.235, that he had written and
handed over a report on atomic research, that he had
also given information about electronic shells and that he
had taken money. He explained that he did not keep the
appointment outside the British Museum about which
he had had instructions from Colonel Zabotin, because
he had *decided that this clandestine procedure was
no longer appropriate in view of the official release of
information and the possibility of satisfactory international control of atomic energy.* He refused to say anything more to the authorities or to help their investigations, and was sentenced to ten years' penal servitude
on May 1st. With the maximum remission for good conduct, he was released on December 30th, 1952, and
the next day declared: "I myself think that I acted
rightly and I believe many others think so too. . . ."

Oddly enough, the Soviet Government was apparently not among those 'others' who thought that

Doctor May had acted rightly. In a statement made in answer to the Canadian Prime Minister's first announcement about the spy-ring, the Russian Foreign Ministry alleged that the information stolen by May and the other spies was "insignificant secret data" and "of no interest" to the Soviet authorities—an extraordinary claim in view of all the trouble and risks that had been taken to obtain it. But the statement also formally admitted the "inadmissability" of the conduct of Colonel Zabotin's staff in Ottawa, and therefore, by implication of May and the other spies.

Meanwhile, in Canada those other spies were standing trial one by one. Zabotin's two chief contact-men, Rose and Carr, were each sentenced to six years in prison, though Carr was not caught and tried until 1949. Lunan, the head of the "B group," and Durnford Smith, its most active member, got five years each; Mazerall and Gerson four, Kathleen Willsher three and Doctor Boyer two. Adams, Benning and Halperin were acquitted.

Altogether, of the twenty persons named by the Royal Commission who were subsequently brought to trial, nine were sentenced to prison by Canadian Courts and one by a British Court; one was fined by a Canadian Court, and nine were found not guilty at their trials.

This was a strange situation. Legal technicalities prevented the Law Courts from hearing much of the evidence which was given to the Commission. And so people who had solemnly been declared to be spies by one authority were then acquitted by another. But the Courts' decisions in no way affected the facts of the case nor the Royal Commission's findings.

Doubtless the Russians were puzzled by "bourgeois" Canadian justice. Probably they were surprised, too, by the lightness of the sentences on those who were condemned. But for Zabotin's Director in the big grey building at 19 Znamensky Street in Moscow it was just another incident. A disagreeable incident, perhaps—but his work went on.

★

The Vavoudes Group

★

By the time that Zabotin's Canadian spies were arrested,
the second world war was over. But for Greece there was
to be fighting for three more years. Civil war, and the bit-
terness and problems it leaves behind, are the background
to the story of the Vavoudes Group.

It is a curious story, partly because of the settings in which
it took place—most of the action was in the underworld of
Athens, but there are glimpses of Paris back-streets, Marseilles docks, the wild, closely guarded northern Greek
frontiers, and communist spy centers in Rumania, Czechoslovakia and Poland—and partly because of the strange and
varied group of men and women who played the leading
parts. There was the tough, uncompromising communist
Central Committee member and his equally bitter mistress;
the wealthy, socially well-connected Admiral's son; the right-
wing journalist; and the score of minor figures—waiters,
sailors, smugglers and a broken-down, small-time actress—
all of them with their own mixed, complicated, and sometimes pathetic, motives for acting as they did.

It is a sinister story, too. It reveals more fully and completely than any other single case, the whole wide range of
communist subversive activity, from the penetration and
control of camouflaged, political "front" movements, through
propaganda and the building-up of a clandestine party network, to straightforward military espionage. In fact, in no
other known case has so great a variety of tasks been undertaken by a single communist spy organization. This was the

135

most unusual feature of the Vavoudes Group. It was also the cause of its eventual downfall.

Afterward, the story of the Vavoudes Group was given various interpretations. In the communist countries, he and some of his colleagues were hailed as martyrs in a brave struggle for liberation, while others of them, apparently no less loyal to their communist masters, were denounced as traitors, police agents and provocateurs. In the democracies, the revelation of their activities was taken in two ways. First, as a harsh, new warning of the need for vigilance. And then as a reminder of the grave dilemma which faces the free peoples: how to preserve intact their democratic liberty without allowing its privileges to be misused by those who work for its destruction.

X

The Two Transmitters

★

Shortly after five o'clock on the afternoon of November 14th, 1951, a 48-year-old Russian-Greek named Nicholas Vavoudes committed suicide. He shot himself in the left temple with a pistol in a smoke-filled Athens cellar. A few hours later he died in the New Ionia hospital nearby. To see in perspective the events which led up to his death, one must first look briefly at the situation in Greece at the time and the problems left by the post-war communist rebellion.

★   ★   ★

No people in Europe outside the Soviet orbit has had such full and varied experience of the technique of communism as the Greeks. In some part of their country, at some period before the early 1950's, practically every weapon in the communist armory has been tried out. And in the ten years after 1940, a communist triumph seemed imminent more than once.

The Greek Communist Party took its present name and shape in 1924 and, for most of the years between the two world wars, it operated freely as a legal political body: fighting and sometimes winning parliamentary seats, infiltrating and controlling parts of the trade union movement, and carrying on an untiring propaganda campaign through its newspapers and its network of party cells. But, like all the other Balkan communist parties except the Bulgarian, it had a hard, slow start. Greek workers—intelligent, well-informed, argumentative and politically fickle—tended to be unreceptive to the rigid discipline and dogma of the communists. The Greek economy, dominated by small peasant landowners, made a poor target for their propaganda. And the Communist Party leadership was torn by incessant quarrels and intrigues which made necessary constant intervention from Moscow and frequent purges.

Many of the Greek communist leaders were trained in Russia. But their other Balkan colleagues thought them excitable and unreliable and tended to be scornful of them and their efforts, so that even the party's leader, Nicholas Zachariades (who in his day was one of the most brilliant pupils of the Lenin School in Moscow), never won much influence in the higher Russian and international communist circles.

The Greek Communist Party's first real opportunity to win mass support came in 1936. That year, general elections gave it fifteen seats and the chance to hold the balance between the two traditional major parties. This precarious parliamentary situation and a series of labor disputes in which communist agitators were active, followed by the threat of a general strike, served as the excuse for a right-wing coup. A dictatorship came to power, and its leader, General John Metaxas, claimed that he had saved Greece from a communist revolution. In reality, the Greek Communist Party was too weak and small to be a serious threat to the established democratic system at that time. But from then on, the unpopularity of the new régime (which was essentially an inefficient and less brutal imitation of German National Socialism and Italian fascism) and the complete disintegration of the democratic political parties made excellent conditions for underground communist activity. The Greek Communist Party, like all other parties, was declared illegal. But of all the Government's opponents, only the communists, with their better understanding of clandestine methods, managed to keep intact a nation-wide organization. They exploited the grievances caused by police persecution; and the official policy of jailing or exiling political suspects exposed some thousands of the régime's most active critics to communist indoctrination. The Communist Party claimed that its militants were turning the prisons and island camps into "universities of Marxism," and the number of party members steadily increased.

In October 1940, Greece entered the second world war. The Metaxas Government bravely defied first Mussolini, then Hitler, with the whole-hearted support of the Greek people, including, it seems, the communists. (In endorsing resistance to the Italian invaders in October 1940—eight months before the German attack on Russia—the Greek communist leaders were apparently out of step, and not for the first time, with their colleagues abroad. But what Moscow thought of this particular deviation is not yet known.)

In the spring of 1941, the Greek armies and the small British forces sent to help them, were defeated by the Germans. Greece was occupied. Then, the miseries of the occupation (whose psychological impact was all the harder because it came so soon after spectacular Greek victories over the Italians in Albania), the inadequacy of successive Greek Governments in exile, and unwise allied policies in occupied Greece, all contributed to help the communists still further. And once again they started with a great practical advantage: they already controlled an organization with cells of experienced clandestine workers throughout the country. On this foundation, soon after the German attack on Russia, they began to build the National Liberation Front: the Greek equivalent of similar communist-led resistance movements that were being formed at the same time throughout occupied Europe.

With substantial British (and later some American) support, but no known practical assistance from the Russians, the EAM (as it was called from its Greek initials) grew large and powerful. It eliminated all rival "national" resistance groups but one, and, toward the end of the occupation, its guerrillas controlled about a third of the Greek mainland and its total membership was variously estimated by British liaison officers on the spot at between two hundred thousand and "a quarter of the whole Greek population." At the beginning, its leaders had emphasized only the patriotic character of the EAM. They canvassed support from Greeks of all parties. But later, when the outcome of the war seemed certain, purely political objectives began to have precedence over military, and straightforward communist and pro-Russian propaganda took the place of the earlier nationalist appeals. At the same time, forced recruiting, the deliberate provocation of German reprisals (in order to "stimulate resistance" in passive villages) and the terrorization of anti-communists became systematic policies in all areas under EAM control. By 1944, the Greek communist leaders confidently expected to make Greece a "People's Democracy" after the war. Perhaps the Russians had kept them inadequately informed of decisions which they had taken at the time of the meetings at Teheran and Yalta; or perhaps Russian policy itself toward Greece was still undecided. But at all events, the Greeks came very near to being drawn behind the Iron Curtain. This was prevented, for the first time, only by British intervention in the 36-day civil war in Athens which ended on January 1st, 1945.

On that day, the defeated EAM leaders signed an agreement with the Greek Government. Their guerrilla army was disbanded, the few remaining prominent non-communists left the EAM and the Greek Communist Party ostensibly became once more an ordinary political movement. *Rizospastes*, its daily paper, appeared again on the newsstands, and a stream of propaganda poured from the party's central office at No. 7 Piraeus Street in Athens. As a purely political force, however, the Greek communists were now seriously weakened. Their atrocities during the civil war—the deportation of civilian hostages, the mass murder and torturing of opponents and suspects—had aroused against them a great wave of popular hatred and fear. But the leadership was not now principally concerned with converting public opinion. Obedient to Lenin's maxim that clandestine, illegal activity must always go side by side with open political campaigning, they were busy reorganizing their defeated followers, building a new underground organization and preparing for another rebellion: the "second round" as they called it. It is at this period that the story of the Vavoudes Group begins.

★   ★   ★

Eight miles south-east of Athens lies the pleasant seaside suburb of Glyphada: a district of neat new villas and wide, tree-lined streets leading down to little beaches and coves and the clear blue water of the Aegean sea. The Villa Avra is a smart, white-painted, five-roomed house with a long, cool veranda, standing in its own quarter-acre garden in a sparsely built-up section of Glyphada near the Chapel of Saint Nicholas.

In March 1946, Avra's owner, Mrs. Avra Moutaphes, let
her house at an annual rent of twenty gold sovereigns,
to a respectable-looking, middle-aged woman called
Domna Papazoglou. Six months later, she raised no
objection when her tenant's place was taken by a thirty-
nine-year-old engineer named Elias Arghyriades who
moved in with his family, explaining that he was Miss
Papazoglou's nephew. He renewed the lease each year,
paid the rising rent promptly, and was polite on the
few occasions when his landlady called to see him.
She saw nothing strange in the fact that he never
asked her to come farther than the veranda. The neighbors, too, had no reason for complaint. In fact, they
rarely saw Arghyriades and his family, who seemed
very quiet people. They seldom left the house during
the day, and apparently had few acquaintances in the
district. Certainly these respectable, middle-class neighbors did not guess that the plump, blonde woman they
knew as Mrs. Arghyriades was not his wife, that the
two young children were illegitimate, that Miss Papazoglou was no relation to Arghyriades but the mistress
of a member of the Central Committee of the Greek
Communist Party, and that Arghyriades himself was a
key member of a spy-ring.

★   ★   ★

Born at Pergamum in Asia Minor, Arghyriades had
been brought to Greece as a child. He made his first
contact with the Communist Party when he was im-
prisoned by the Metaxas Government for his activities
in the trade unions, and he had joined the party in 1937.
During the occupation, both he and his mistress, Catherine Dallas, had served with the EAM guerrillas, and
he had been arrested in Athens during the communist
rebellion. Early in 1945, having finally abandoned his

wife, he set up home with his mistress, living for a time on the premises of the Communist Party's central office in Piraeus Street, where he worked as a watchman.

In the summer of 1946, Arghyriades was suddenly sent for by the Party's General Secretary, Nicholas Zachariades, who ordered him to move into the Villa Avra. At the same time, he told Domna Papazoglou (who had originally rented it on party instructions) to move out. Arghyriades took Catherine Dallas and the children with him and, soon afterwards, they were joined by two more trusted communists: a young brother and sister—children of a dead Central Committee member—named Philaretos and Roula Lazarides. These two explained their presence in the house by saying that Arghyriades was their uncle. Meanwhile, with money provided by the Communist Party, Arghyriades started a chicken farm for two thousand birds at nearby Terpsithea, as a cover for his new, moderately prosperous way of life.

Then, when the four subordinates had settled in and it was clear that no suspicions had been aroused, Zachariades himself called at the Villa Avra and brought with him the man he had selected as chief of the new spy-ring.

*   *   *

Nicholas Vavoudes was born at Odessa in Russia in 1903. He arrived in Greece as a refugee in the mid-twenties and was jailed in the early thirties for his part in the murder of a policeman, by which time, it seems, he was already an active Communist Party member. But in May 1934 he broke out of Aegina prison with a group of other communists, boarded a Soviet ship, the *Novorossisk*, which was in Greek waters nearby, and escaped to Russia. There he received special training in clandestine work before returning unobtrusively to Greece. His next known assignment was as personal wireless operator to Colonel Popov, the chief of the Soviet Military Mission which arrived at the headquarters of the EAM guerrillas during the later stages of the occupation. When the war ended Vavoudes went underground. Nothing more was known of him, except by his communist associates, for the next six years.

Meanwhile, however, in the summer of 1946, those associates and he were busy fitting up the cellar of the Villa Avra as a secret wireless transmitter station. To cover their building operations, they asked their landlady, the unsuspecting Mrs. Moutaphes, for permission to make a new chicken house in a corner of the garden. In this way, attention was diverted from the cellar while they tunnelled out a hiding-place among the foundations of the building. In a few weeks their work was done. Cleverly concealed under the basement washhouse sink was an entrance, closed from the inside by a concrete block sliding on two rails, which led to two small rooms, one behind the other: the first was about ten feet square, the second slightly larger. A hidden cable led up from the inner room to an ordinary-looking radio aerial outside the house. Electric light, heat and power were installed and a small, reserve, paraffin-burning generator was put in. Meanwhile two small but powerful wireless transmitters were brought to the new hideout. Arghyriades fetched the first from the Communist Party central office, and Vavoudes brought the second. One was a wartime British set camouflaged in a brown leather suitcase; the other had been assembled from American components. The range of either set was not less than seven hundred miles.

★   ★   ★

From the Villa Avra, the scene now moves to a small, square, red-tiled artisan's house in the untidy Athens working-class district of Callithea. Number 39 Lycurgus Street was empty. A vine straggled in the yard behind the house and dust swirled against the closed brown shutters. The owner, Maria Solomos, had been active with the communist guerrillas during the occupation and her brother, an old Communist Party member, was living in Brazil. But she was now less concerned with politics than with her property. She was waiting hopefully for a tenant for her house. In May 1946 her hopes were answered. A simple-looking, grey-haired old carpenter named Nicholas Caloumenos rented the house for himself, his wife Urania, his two daughters, seventeen-year-old Margaret and Mary who was then just sixteen, and his six-year-old son Peter. They seemed quiet people, showed no interest in politics and kept themselves discreetly to themselves. Each morning they took the *Ethnikos Kiryx*, a stoutly right-wing daily. In a place of honor in their sitting-room they hung a picture of the King and Queen of Greece. At Callithea high school, Mary recited patriotic speeches. The neighbors gave little thought to the Caloumenos family, and the local police—who, because of the landlord's record, had watched the house—noted them as people most unlikely to give trouble. It seems doubtful whether even Maria Solomos herself thought of them as anything but careful tenants.

This was precisely the impression it was intended that they should make. For Nicholas Caloumenos was another key man in the Vavoudes spy-ring.

*   *   *

A Greek from Calymnus in the Dodecanese islands, Caloumenos had gone as a young man to Constantinople in Turkey and had there become an active communist and also, for a time after the Russian revolution, had acted as a minor Soviet agent. It was at this period that he first met Nicholas Zachariades, who was then also in Constantinople. But in 1922 he was arrested by the Turkish police and sent to forced labor at Zonguldak on the Black Sea. From there he escaped to Russia where, according to his own later account, he was sent for a year to a rest home in the Crimea. In 1926 he came to Greece and from then on, as far as is known, was politically inactive. He himself claimed that his only contact with the Communist Party was when he was asked to make coffins for its dead during the 1944 civil war in Athens. But at all events, he had not been forgotten by the party leaders. Zachariades sent for him in the spring of 1946, and it was he who told Caloumenos to take the house at Callithea, and the Communist Party which paid the rent. The purpose of the move was to provide a second secret wireless transmitter station for the use of Nicholas Vavoudes.

Once again, an underground crypt was carefully prepared and two more transmitters were installed: a second set assembled from American components and a brand new Russain model. The old carpenter was a clever craftsman and the hiding-place was well concealed. It was, in fact, far safer than the cellar at the Villa Avra. Even to a person standing directly on it, there was no sign that the stone step leading from the kitchen to the yard could be lifted out to make a secret entrance, then firmly bolted back into position from underneath. Down below, an electric fan kept air moving in the stuffy crypt. A red light, controlled from above, could flash a danger warning. There was space for two beds and there was a ventilator shaft which also could be used to pass messages or small objects from the room above. Elsewhere in his house, Caloumenos made smaller hiding-places: a cupboard with a false bottom, a sliding panel above a doorway and several other inconspicuous niches for messages and papers.

★   ★   ★

Meanwhile other houses were being made ready in the Athens area for the use of the Vavoudes Group, and unobtrusive meeting-places arranged in small shops and cafés and private homes throughout the city. At the same time, similar but quite separate subversive groups were being set up both in the capital and in other parts of Greece. For this was a period of planning and preparation for the Greek communists. Their task was relatively easy. Despite the violent public reaction against them and despite some persecution by the police, particularly out in the countryside, they still had their big legal party organization as a cover, and they still had big sums of money—mostly in British gold sovereigns—saved from the wartime funds dropped by the Allies to the EAM. Even the anti-communist police action, such as it was, probably helped them more than it hindered: for it was often the simple ex-guerrilla or the local rank-and-file party member who got into trouble with the village gendarme, while the militants and organizers—the men who really were a danger— took care to make themselves inconspicuous, or to pose as anti-communist stalwarts, while they busied themselves with preparations for the future.

The first messages from Vavoudes' transmitters were probably sent at the end of 1946. At that time, he used them mainly as a quick, safe channel of communication between the Greek party leadership in Athens and secret communist stations at Skoplje in Yugoslavia and Sofia in Bulgaria. He moved at will from the Villa Avra to Lycurgus Street. At the Villa, he successfully trained the slim, 19-year-old Roula Lazarides as an assistant wireless operator and meanwhile made her his mistress. At the Caloumenos house, he often took young Mary down into his crypt where he made love to her too. But his efforts to teach her to use his transmitters were unsuccessful and her mother complained at the long hours she was spending in his dark, airless hideout.

★   ★   ★

Meanwhile, outside Athens a second communist rebellion was now brewing. A few small scattered parties of former EAM guerrillas had remained up in the hills ever since the occupation, occasionally raiding an isolated village, shooting a gendarme or kidnapping some peasant boy as a new recruit. They were a nuisance to the people of the remote areas where they operated, but little worse. But now, big new guerrilla bands sprang up throughout the country. They turned for support, which was promptly given, to the satellite countries behind Greece's northern frontiers: to Albania, Yugoslavia and Bulgaria. From those neighbors supplies, arms and ammunition began to reach them. Then, in the autumn of 1947, Zachariades and the remaining leaders of the Greek Communist Party in Athens suddenly disappeared. Soon afterwards they announced their solidarity with the guerrillas' "Democratic Army" which formally pledged itself to "liberate" Greece and ally her with the Soviet Union, and claimed that they had set up a "Democratic Government" in the mountains. In reply, on December 27th, the Greek Government outlawed the Communist Party, closed its offices, suspended its newspaper and arrested all those active members whom it could trace. The Vavoudes Group assumed a new importance.

The transmitters at the Villa Avra and Lycurgus Street were now mostly used for signalling to guerrilla units inside Greece, giving them news of Greek army movements and of developments at Athens. But since July 1947 they had also taken on another important job. In that month, copying Allied wartime propaganda methods, the communists set up a Greek-speaking "Freedom Radio" which claimed to be operating from Greek soil but was actually then located in southern Yugoslavia. *Radio Free Greece* depended largely on the Vavoudes Group for a quick and regular supply of Greek news. So the Group was gradually expanded, and three new reserve transmitters were established in houses in other sections of the city.

For the next two years, the guerrilla war raged in the mountains. But in June 1947 American aid, sent under the Truman Doctrine, started reaching Greece. In July 1948 Marshal Tito broke with the Cominform and, soon afterwards, sealed the Yugoslav-Greek border, cutting the main supply lines of the guerrillas. In the summer of 1949, the Greek Army won crushing victories at Vitsi and Grammos in the north of Greece. The remnants of the "Democratic Army" fled for sanctuary to Albania and Bulgaria, the party leaders went into the exile with them, and the second civil war was over. The story of the Vavoudes Group had entered its final phase. Until now, it would have been possible (though rather fanciful) to claim that it had been merely an intelligence and propaganda service of a rebel army. But the Greek communists themselves had probably long foreseen the failure of their second effort to seize power, and had expected Vavoudes to do his most useful work after its defeat. During the last months of the fighting in 1949 their policy became something of a puzzle. To the outside observer it even seemed that they, or their Russian masters, had deliberately decided that the collapse of the "Democratic Army" must be made as complete and as spectacular as possible, and had given orders to that end. One can find no other logical explanation for the suicidal military tactics adopted by the guerrillas during the final stages of the civil war, nor for the circumstances in which the rebel commander "General" Markos was dismissed and denounced for treachery and deviation. But by then, of course, the growing power of the Greek Army, Marshal Tito's defection and American aid had made the guerrillas' defeat inevitable in any case.

At all events, the Vauvodes Group, intact and undisturbed by the disasters round it, now became one of the principal instruments left to the communists in Greece. For the next two years it served them well.

XI

Vavoudes Breaks the Rules

★

At the final collapse of the "Democratic Army" in the late summer of 1949, some thirty thousand Greek communists fled across the northern frontiers. Their rebellion had cost Greece more than one hundred thousand dead, it had made over a million people temporarily homeless and it had caused about three hundred and sixty million dollars' worth of material damage—all this in a country with a total population of less than eight millions. The Communist Party itself was in a state of disintegration. Inside Greece, it hardly existed except for its various small, subversive organizations, like the Vavoudes Group, which had been set up beforehand to meet just such a situation. Almost all the important party leaders had fled with the guerrillas: the Central Committee had left only three senior representatives in Athens and of these one was shot a few months later and another was summoned behind the Iron Curtain. There remained only Nicholas Ploumbides, a fifty-year-old party veteran, trained in Moscow, who had been a member of the Greek Politbureau since 1932 but was now suffering from tuberculosis.

In exile, the party's Central Committee went through another period of dissension and recrimination. Severely disciplined by Moscow, it indulged in an orgy of "self-criticism" and expelled and denounced a number of its leading members as deviationists, traitors, and fascist spies. It then turned to the task of rebuilding its shattered forces inside Greece. Although, at the time of their military defeat, the Greek communist leaders proclaimed that this was only a temporary setback and threatened that there would soon be a new call to arms, they evidently realized that in fact there would be no possibility of another rebellion for many years, and that meanwhile Greece would stay outside the Iron Curtain. Without doubt, they also expected that the Communist Party would remain illegal inside Greece, though they probably did not foresee how soon tolerant Greek governments would allow communist propaganda to be freely carried on behind the mask of new political "front" organizations.

The Greek communist leaders were given ample help by the communist governments of the satellite countries where they took refuge. Most of the guerrillas who had escaped across the frontiers were gradually transported to Rumania, Hungary, Czechoslovakia and Poland, where the majority of them were absorbed as unskilled labor. But a minority of the more militant communists among them were selected, by representatives of the Greek Central Committee, for training in subversive work, before being sent back secretly to Greece. At special schools near Warsaw, Prague and Budapest and in other places, they were given intensive courses in such subjects as wireless telegraphy, cryptography, photography, clandestine organization and sabotage. Then they were sent south, usually through Sofia in Bulgaria, to be smuggled singly or in small groups, and sometimes with wireless transmitters, across the border. Many of them were captured in the frontier areas; some at once surrendered, and from them the Greek authorities learned a great deal about communist espionage techniques. But these men were all very minor characters. Infiltration across the frontier was too dangerous a route for really valuable agents. They were sent by air direct to Athens, travelling in disguise and with false passports.

★   ★   ★

It was in this way that, in June, 1950, two senior members of the Central Committee returned to Greece: Nicholas Belogiannes and Nicholas Akritides. Of the movements of Belogiannes, both before and after his arrival, a great deal was later learned. But the brief appearance in this story of Akritides is still part of an unsolved mystery: even the fact that it is known that he came to Athens—where he was probably still working, undetected, several years later—is due to a blunder on his part so extraordinary and so unlikely that it deserves a brief account.

Towards the end of June, a stranger, holding a passport of a South American Republic, booked in at the Grand Hotel in Constitution Square in the center of Athens. After a short stay he vanished, leaving in his room a suitcase and some clothes. When he failed to return to claim them, the hotel management gave them in as lost property to the Athens city police. As they were being listed a policeman found in the pocket of a suit a numbered ticket which, from the writing on it, showed that it had been handed to a passer-by by a street photographer in Rome. The Athens police sent the ticket to their Italian colleagues, who traced the photographer, developed the photograph to which the ticket referred and forwarded it to Athens. It was a clear and unmistakable portrait of Nicholas Akritides, one-time head of the communist youth movement and a former "Minister" in the rebel "Government" during the civil war, of whose whereabouts, until that moment, the Greek police had known nothing. But all further efforts to trace him failed.

His colleague, Belogiannes, was less lucky. He was arrested just six months later, his mission to reorganize the underground Greek Communist Party uncompleted. This was a task for which he was well qualified. A sturdy, tough young man from southern Greece, he had already spent eighteen of his thirty-four years as a party member, and had served a prison sentence before the war. During the occupation, he was political commissar to the EAM guerrillas in the Peloponnese, and a member of his party's "Control Commission," the body which supervises the loyalty of other members. In 1947 he went to northern Greece, became a Lieutenant-Colonel in the guerrilla army, was in charge of security at EAM headquarters and, in January 1949, directed an attack on the small Macedonian town of Naoussa during which 360 citizens were killed, 580 were wounded, 600 were taken as hostages, the Mayor was shot in the main square and every factory building was destroyed. Seven months later, he fled behind the Iron Curtain and later went to Poland, where he took a course at an espionage school near Warsaw. On his return to Athens in 1950, he at once made contact with Nicholas Vavoudes. It was the Vavoudes Group which found him safe lodgings in the city, provided him with money, sent wireless messages for him to Bucharest and delivered to him, in return, answers and instructions.

Belogiannes' task was party organization. He was senior to Vavoudes—who, incidentally, resented his arrival. He used the Vavoudes Group at his convenience, but chiefly as a channel of communication. The Group itself, however, was already fully occupied with other work.

★   ★   ★

Apart from reorganizing its own membership inside
Greece, the Greek Communist Party at this time had
three main aims. First, to intensify its propaganda. Second, to develop its political activity under cover of
fellow-travelling, but legal, "front" organizations. And
finally to carry out military espionage in the interests
of Russia and of the satellite governments who, for this
purpose, were giving the Greek Communist leaders in
exile considerable practical help.

It is, of course, quite contrary to the most elementary
rules of espionage for such a variety of work to be handled by one single group. Above all, agents engaged in
spying ought never to become involved in politics or
propaganda. Why did Vavoudes continue for so long
to break these rules? Probably there are several answers.
By nature, the Greek communists seem to be less efficient in such matters than their comrades in other countries. Besides, they had just suffered total military
defeat and a large proportion of their reliable members
were either suspects or in prison or abroad. Finally, in
this case, unlike the others described in detail in this
book, the Group was being operated by remote control
—by wireless from a distant country—and ostensibly at
least, only by Greeks. So far as is known, members of
the Group had no direct, personal contact with Russians.
So the consequences, if it should be discovered, were
less grave. At worst, the Group would be destroyed and
a few party members would lose their lives, to serve as
object lessons to other communists in heroism or care-
lessness, as the case might be. One must add, however,
that Vavoudes himself was aware of the defects of

his organization and sent many messages suggesting changes to Bucharest.

*   *   *

But meanwhile he and his associates were busy with their triple task: propaganda, the creation of a political "front" organization and military espionage.

By this time his Group had grown to a considerable size. In Athens alone he had some dozens of contact-men, informers and spies. There were agents in the civil service and the armed forces, and reports reached him from all parts of Greece. Though they were all recruited from among Communist Party members and sympathizers, many of his helpers were regularly paid. Money was needed, too, for rent for the houses where he worked his transmitters, and to maintain himself and those of his assistants—like Arghyriades and the brother and sister Lazarides—most or all of whose working time was given to the Group. And, though Vavoudes often complained that he was kept dangerously short, money did reach him regularly and in big amounts. At times his expenditure was as much as about twenty thousand dollars a month. With such large sums at his disposal Vavoudes felt justified in a little personal extravagance at times. Life at the Villa Avra was not austere, and once (according to his colleague Arghyriades), when he spent nearly thirty dollars on a single evening's outing, he boasted: "We are the aristocrats of the party now."

But by now the communists had run short of ready money inside Greece. Their hoard of British sovereigns had been spent, and it became necessary to smuggle gold and dollars from foreign countries. To supply Vavoudes and their other agents with these smuggled funds, they set up a special organization in Athens with connections in Western Europe. At its head was a young lawyer named Demetrius Batses, the son of an aged and respected Admiral. In Athens society, Batses was known as a wealthy, left-wing intellectual. During the occupation he had interested himself in a study-group concerned with post-war planning called 'Science and Reconstruction,' at first a non-political body which had later been penetrated by the Communist Party. He also published an economic and technological magazine, *Antaios*. These activities were treated light-heartedly by Batses' rich Athenian friends when they met him at parties or visited him in his expensive flat in Heracleiou Street. They joked of his success with women, commiserated when he divorced his first wife, Lena Ailianos, the daughter of a leading Conservative politician, and congratulated him when, soon afterwards, he married the beautiful twenty-four-year-old Lilian Calamaro, whose father was a prosperous Italian business man.

The smooth appearance and the rather ineffectual manner of a spoiled Athenian playboy were excellent cover for Batses in his dangerous work. It was to him, through intermediaries and cut-out men, that secret couriers brought belts of gold coins and packages of bank-notes, and it was he who distributed the money to Vavoudes and other communist agents in Athens. Most of his funds came from France, where at that time, Miltiades Porphyrogenes, the member of the Greek Communist Party's Central Committee who was allegedly responsible for finance, happened to be living. Sometimes the money was carried by foreigners: two Frenchwomen and a Swiss are known to have made journeys for Batses. Occasionally a Greek traveller would be used, like the actress Maria Callerghi. The daughter of a Greek café proprietor who had settled in France, Callerghi returned to Greece after his death and lived there through the occupation. After the liberation, she went back to Paris to study dramatics and there became the mistress of Panagiotes Demetracareas, an old Communist Party member who was also, surprisingly, the Paris correspondent of the right-wing Athens daily *Ethnikos Kiryx*. He persuaded her to smuggle funds to Greece, and she made several journeys for him.

But most of Batses' foreign money was carried to him by Greek seamen working on ships which plied between Marseilles and Piraeus, the port of Athens. The Communist Party had for long been active in the Greek Seamen's Union, which it had used extensively for recruiting volunteers during the civil war. Most of the men the communists now employed as smugglers were therefore already known to them. But they usually paid them for their work, often offering them a percentage of each consignment they delivered. More than once, however, part or all of the money went astray. To a deckhand or a steward, whatever his political convictions, a leather belt stuffed with three or four hundred sovereigns was a powerful temptation. And so anxious messages were often exchanged between Vavoudes and his masters in Bucharest on the subject of missing funds. Vavoudes once asked whether it would not be possible for money to be sent through the banks, camouflaged as commercial transfers (a method often used in other countries), but Bucharest answered that this could not be done. In September 1950, they sent this message:

We are much worried by the money question. We are now sending another ten thousand via Batses even though five thousand have been lost and all evidence indicates that they reached Athens. What happened after that we do not know. We are taking action also from elsewhere.

About commercial transfers, our people tell us that it cannot be done because commercial transfers have stopped. . . .

From the sovereigns you save, give fifty to Belogiannes with an order that he uses them only for his personal needs and report to us.

A little later Vavoudes wirelessed:

From Batses we have taken all seven thousand. Ploumbides kept one thousand. Once again we have no money.

To this Bucharest replied:

. . . You say you received altogether seven thousand. Please clarify this matter. We sent nine thousand, why did you receive seven thousand?

Two days later Vavoudes answered:

Batses has sent the account to Ploumbides. It was you who told the man who brought it to keep 10,500,000 (i.e. Greek drachmae: a sum then worth about $500).

In October 1951, Vavoudes was again complaining:

. . . Batses says your man went regularly to his house without money. Then a girl arrived to deliver the money and fixed a day and time to come and deliver the money but she did not bring the money nor reappear. Take steps to send us money at once. I have not a penny to give anyone. My group is in a dangerous state. Without money we can do nothing. You should know that if anything happens to me the main reason will be because I am constantly penniless.

But Batses was not the only channel through which money reached the Vavoudes Group. A message from Bucharest in the summer of 1950 said:

I have at your disposal 20,000 dollars. We could dispatch them in one month and a half. If you have a means of receiving them sooner, inform me at once. . . .

Batses himself afterwards claimed that he had only
started handling money for the Communist Party in
September 1950 and that the total which had passed
through his hands was a little over 450 million drachmae ($22,000); whereas the expenditure of the Vavou-
des Group was sometimes more than this sum in six
weeks. How the balance of Vavoudes' funds reached
him is still not known.

★   ★   ★

Meanwhile, his transmitters were busily at work. A
large proportion of his messages were devoted to what
Vavoudes himself called "the Agency": a daily service
of Greek news, background information and political
comment, on which the exiled Communist Party propa-
gandists based their output. Their chief instrument was
still *Radio Free Greece* which, in 1948, had moved to
Bucharest. Its programs were easily heard throughout
Greece and were an excellent means of keeping sympathizers informed of the current party line, spreading
rumors and waging a war of nerves. And, thanks to the
Vavoudes Group, its news bulletins were sometimes so
up to date that it must have been hard for the ordinary
listener not to wonder whether they were not, in fact,
broadcast from inside Greece.

For his "Agency" work, Vavoudes relied partly on the
Athens press, partly on Communist Party members and
partly on paid informers. His messages regularly included comments on topical events, details of strikes
and other signs of social unrest, reports on any communist activity that might have taken place, and attacks
on the Americans and British in Greece.

On October 21st, 1950, Vavoudes reported:

. . . *In support of the strike of seven currant-workers'
unions, dockers of Calamata, loading officials, watch-*

*men, lightermen, porters and maintenance workers have
struck. The port is paralyzed. Four ships left unloaded.
400 tons of currants sent by motor boats from Patras.*

On December 17th, he wirelessed:

*Week's chief feature is violent anti-communist hys-
teria. War preparations and oppression growing. Arrest
of ten demonstrators and trials for sabotage are obvious
provocation. War preparations caused panic to popu-
lations of Macedonia, Epirus, even Thessaly. Athens
completely panicked. Everyone hoarding sovereigns.
On December 8th Bank (i.e. of Greece) sold ninety
thousand sovereigns owing to Truman's statement on
use of* (atomic) *bomb, etc. Palace and Americans preparing new Government.*

Each week Vavoudes added a summary of prices,
exchange rates and the cost of living index, to compile
which Arghyriades went regularly into Athens from the
Villa Avra. His signal for December 13th reported:

. . . *General retail 399–8. Foodstuffs 406–15. Paper
pound 41,440. Dollar 16,060. Maize 3,000. Rice 9,000.
Oil 17,800.*

Apart from material for their broadcasts, the propa-
gandists of *Radio Free Greece* also relied on Vavoudes'
"Agency" for comments and advice. On September 16th,
1950, they asked:

*Belogiannes should tell us the following. How many
transmissions of our radio station do you need and for
how many hours? That is to say, we can change our
transmission times and add other transmissions. All
these changes will be made only on your recommenda-
tion. Therefore we await considered suggestions which
will enable us to go ahead. . . .*

But sometimes the advice they got from Athens was
very vague and unspecific. On October 19th Vavoudes
merely asked:

Please study and do your best for radio station in every way to encourage morale and inspire faith in victory and increase fighting spirit of party members and fighters. In this way war of nerves and attacks of Monarcho-Fascism (the term usually used by communists to describe non-communist Greeks) *will be more successfully met.*

The Vavoudes Group, however, did not confine its propaganda mission to sending information to Bucharest. They were also busy producing printed pamphlets for distribution by communists in Athens, for which purpose Vavoudes began to buy stocks of paper and installed in the cellar of the Villa Avra a small printing press which Roula Lazarides learned to work. But he also had other, more ambitious plans. On February 25th, 1951, he signalled:

. . . I must rent six houses in Athens and Piraeus to organize the leaflets as I wrote to you. Each house will have its own small printing press and supplies for one year, so that it can distribute 30,000 200-word leaflets every fifteen days. Houses will depend directly on your station (i.e. *Radio Free Greece*) *and you will give the slogans. They will have no contact with anyone and will not know each other. I already have stocks for five million leaflets. I also have two houses but am not going ahead in order to collect all stocks needed for one year because they might cut us off. I estimate that if I have money I can start work in two months at latest. . . .*

But distributing communist literature by hand in the Athens streets was a risky job, so Vavoudes tried a more imaginative method. On June 6th, he reported:

We continue trial dropping of leaflets. We fill balloons with hydrogen. We tie the leaflets underneath. We light a fuse and arrange for it to burn the string in however many minutes and at whatever height we want. The leaf-

lets fall on the streets, yards and balconies. Only obstacle is that these days wind blew in opposite direction to what we needed and the leaflets would have fallen on the fields. I am now arranging houses so that we can drop irrespective of direction of wind.

These experiments were made at night and do not seem, in the end, to have been successful.

★   ★   ★

More than once, Vavoudes claimed that his "Agency" and propaganda work were taking up too much time and making it hard for him to give enough attention to his other activities. Of those activities, the part which caused the biggest sensation in Athens when it was eventually revealed was the efforts—very successful efforts—to create a "front" which could be used by the still illegal Communist Party as a cover for a new public political campaign.

In September 1951, a general parliamentary election was held in Greece. For weeks beforehand, Vavoudes was handling a mass of detailed messages giving orders from the exiled Communist Party leadership on the tactics to be followed by its representatives in Athens in building up a new party—the United Democratic Left, known by its Greek initials EDA—which could take part in the elections. The original leaders of EDA were ostensibly left-wing non-communists. But in fact, the exiled communist leaders in Bucharest had complete control from the beginning. They dictated EDA's election program in great detail, they chose the candidates and they even decided the new party's name and slogans. On August 8th they wirelessed:

We await information on progress of Democratic left . . . Ploumbides must intervene energetically and directly. He must make it an absolute condition that

*candidates in all constituencies shall be well-known im-
prisoned or exiled fighters. . . .*

*EDA's program is clear: Peace—Democracy—Amnesty
and the rest which you know and which our radio station* (i.e. *Radio Free Greece*) *broadcasts. You must act
energetically and take your line from our radio. EDA
must understand that, if it does not accept our pro-
posals, we shall openly denounce it. . . .*

Three days later, Vavoudes sent back this answer
from Ploumbides:

*EDA's slogan is Peace—Democracy—Amnesty. I have
fixed their line and told them to amend their program
and to put up candidates we propose, choosing prisoners and exiles. I threatened we would attack anyone
who goes against the people.*

For the next ten days scores of new messages arrived
from Bucharest listing the names of candidates who
should be put forward in the various constituencies. Ten
of these men were in fact elected. All ten were communists who were serving terms of imprisonment or deportation by the Government.

Meanwhile the party leaders in Bucharest had decided that the new Party must have a newspaper,
directed, controlled and subsidized by them. (Ploumbides) *must insist absolutely that the newspaper appears at once,* they ordered on August 20th; and, on
August 25th, *Tell us immediately our* [sic] *newspaper
appears and send us whatever comments there are
about its publication.* Four days later they asked: *If the
newspaper has appeared yet, send us a summary of
contents.* The following day, Vavoudes announced: *The
first number of* Democrates *has been in terrific demand
throughout the country.* A little later, he reported the
circulation figures. But *Democrates,* it seems, was running at a loss. *Do not worry, we are sending money for*

the newspaper . . . said a message from Bucharest on October 26th. And six days later they informed Vavoudes of further arrangements they had made to help: *We are arranging for correspondents from all the Peoples' Democracies for the newspaper. Rumania will file press cables, etc., to the paper's office with the signature Radia Han.*

On November 9th, seven of the successful EDA candidates were brought to Athens while the validity of their election, as prisoners, was discussed by the appropriate courts. Five days earlier, Vavoudes had asked: *The exiled members are arriving. I have arranged for them to be briefed and to take control of the EDA newspapers. When that is done, is my mission finished?*

What reply his leaders sent him, or whether they ever congratulated him and his colleague Ploumbides on their work, is not known. But certainly they had every reason to be pleased. To create a complete political party, establish a newspaper and run a nation-wide election campaign from a foreign capital 500 miles away was, at the least, a remarkable achievement—particularly since, at the time, EDA's opponents, whatever their suspicions, could produce no concrete evidence of foreign control, whereas fellow-travelling leaders of EDA could (and did) reject the suggestion, with self-righteous indignation, as "lying, anti-democratic propaganda."

*   *   *

The third and most serious part of the mission of the Vavoudes Group was military espionage. There is as yet no direct evidence to show for precisely which intelligence department of which foreign government or governments this work was undertaken, and the reader must draw his own conclusions. But it is clear that the information collected by Vavoudes' military spies was of no political interest whatever to the Greek Communist Party or, for that matter, to any other non-military organization. Perhaps it passed through various hands behind the Iron Curtain before it reached its ultimate destination. At all events it was regarded as a major part of the work of Vavoudes' Group, and a high proportion of his reports were devoted to military matters.

For example, on December 17th, 1950, he reported: *On small islands between Rhodes and the Turkish coast, big installations for Superforts and submarines. Underground tunnels and depots. Only Turkish labor under American supervision.* On February 4th, 1951: *The harbor of Portoraphtes is being prepared for landings.* On March 5th: *Underground magazines built under Metaxas at Stylis being repaired and war material taken there. All army workshops have left Salonica for Larissa. River Calamas area in Epirus fortified and mines laid. Area considered military zone and no movements there without permission of military authorities.* On May 20th: *Fortification works constructed on Chalcidice isthmus. 24th (or 44th) regiment stationed at Serres. 303 battalion at West of Beles and 74 East. The valley of Istimbey is unguarded. Be careful as this may be a trap.* (Mount Beles is on the Bulgarian border. Perhaps the last sentence was a warning to the organizers who smuggled agents into Greece.) On June 24th: *At Goudi the ammunition magazines are four meters below ground. Five kilometers southeast of Megara opposite Pagia island is a hill in which many separate explosive magazines have been dug. Between Megara and the hill is an airfield where training aircraft land.* On July 7th: *Armored units located at following places. Volos 393 regiment. At Amynteon two regiments. At Salonica and at Menidi near Athens. At Philadelphia* (an Athens sub-

urb) *a unit called armored assault squadron with a
strength of 200 men. . . .*

There were scores of similar messages, some of them
giving positions of fortifications or military units, others
details of equipment, weapons and ammunition. But
often Bucharest asked for more. *Send us more information and news,* they signalled on March 7th, 1951. *Do
you know what the Army Council discussed at its last
session?* And on March 17th: *Send us all you can about
the latest changes in the high command. . . . Find out
also what units compose the army group in Central
Greece. . . .*

★   ★   ★

During 1950 and 1951, the Vavoudes Group was
working at great pressure. Vavoudes himself often
found it hard to keep up with the flood of instructions
and inquiries from Bucharest. His transmitters were on
the air dangerously often, and for too long at a time for
safety. He was also worried (and quite rightly) at the
fact that his Group was combining Communist Party
liaison, political work, propaganda and military espionage. He complained particularly that the "Agency"—
his information bulletins for *Radio Free Greece*—inter-
fered with his other duties. On December 13th, 1950,
he sent a suggestion for a complete reorganization.

*I propose the wireless work be divided into three
parts.*

*First, party liaison. I will give Belogiannes three sets
to have contact with you once weekly to handle party
signals. He can also act as reserve.*

*Second, the Agency which will work daily as soon
as I receive money. . . .*

*Third, I will keep the sets which give information
(i.e. espionage).*

If you agree, inform Belogiannes.

It seems that by now, Vavoudes had several new transmitters at his disposal; and he was discussing with Bucharest a plan to use an automatic morse sender with one of them, for his agency bulletins—though whether it was actually ever used is not known. But his plans for a reorganization at this time were disturbed (as the next chapter shows) by an unforeseen event exactly one week later.

In the following spring, he was again worried, and made new suggestions for changes in the organization of his Group. On April 23rd, 1951, he wirelessed:

Information network . . . is not giving the results it should. . . . To establish, organize and expand, we should spend at least some ten millions (about $500) *a month for houses, wages, and travel expenses. Reply whether you approve. . . .*

As soon as I receive money, both the information agency and my wireless will become mobile because as we are working now they will catch us. . . .

But it seems that the reorganization was never carried out because, for the next six months of 1951, his own transmitters at the Villa Avra and Lycurgus Street continued to handle, in growing volume, messages which covered the same variety of tasks as he had been dealing with before.

His message of November 5th, about the arrival of the EDA candidates in Athens, had ended with the words: *is my mission finished?* It seems that, actually, he was referring only to the political negotiations with EDA. But though he did not know it, his mission was indeed nearly at an end. The risks he had been running for so long had caught up with him. Nine days later, he was dead.

XII

Heroes and Traitors

*

The first trouble happened in the autumn of 1947. Elias Arghyriades, Vavoudes' chief assistant at the Villa Avra, was arrested. But, as it turned out, this had no connection with his illegal work. The second civil war had started in the mountains and the Greek government were making a general roundup of suspects. As a Communist Party member known to have been active in the past, Arghyriades was deported to the island of Icaria. But, by the simple expedient of asking for and signing a formal declaration renouncing communism, he soon secured his release, and returned to the Villa Avra where he found everything in order. He told Vavoudes of the declaration and his chief said that he had acted wisely. There were no repercussions. But Arghyriades took the precaution of becoming acquainted with one of the local gendarmes, who was the only person in the neighborhood with whom he occasionally spent an evening. Precisely what their relations were is still not clear.

The next mishap was much more serious. On December 17th, 1950, Vavoudes received two urgent messages from Bucharest. The first read:

145 if you have a transmitter in Phalerum area or Voula, take immediate action because it is in imminent danger.

A few hours later this was followed by:

Our 145. Answer immediately whether you have transmitters in places we indicated and whether you took effective action.

These warnings prove, incidentally, that Vavoudes' masters had other, speedy channels of information in the Athens area besides his Group. What steps he took for his protection are not known, but three days later his superior, Nicholas Belogiannes, was arrested and three days after that the police caught Belogiannes' mistress, Elli Ioannides, a prominent Communist Party member who had, at times, acted as go-between for delivering money for Demetrius Batses. She and Belogiannes were held for trial under a law which forbade attempts to revive the Greek Communist Party, but the police learned nothing from them about the Vavoudes Group.

There was evidently another scare early in 1951, for on February 20th Vavoudes sent a message signed by the code number of Ploumbides.

Carrying out your orders have stopped all work, activity and contact. From the money I found in Belogiannes' house, I gave Rizo (the Communist Party's illegal newspaper Rizopastes) *enough for three months. With my own funds I cannot come abroad. You arrange. I declare I will shut myself up and not leave my house and shall be at your disposal at any moment for anything whatever.*

To this message, Vavoudes himself added:

Ploumbides told me: tell the boys that this complete isolation has very much upset me.

Whatever the trouble was, however, it soon subsided. For that summer, Ploumbides was again in constant contact with the Vavoudes Group, and—as has already been told—he was extremely busy, as Athens representative of the exiled communist leaders, organizing EDA for the elections.

It was while he was busy with the elections that another dangerous event occurred. Information had reached the police at Piraeus that large sums in gold and dollars were being smuggled into Greece. They arrested a ship's steward carrying a consignment of British sovereigns from Marseilles. Investigations followed and some further arrests were made. To the surprise of the police, they began to build up evidence which pointed unmistakably at the Admiral's son, Demetrius Batses. From mid-June, he had been living (rather surprisingly) in a fourth-class Glyphada hotel called the International, not far from the Villa Avra. Here he had rented a small suite of rooms for four months, although he was sometimes absent for several days at a time and often went out late at night. The police began to shadow Batses. But Batses' communist associates had taken the precaution of providing him with a bodyguard of their own: a former EAM guerrilla who had himself once been a policeman, named Phoustanos. This man noticed that Batses was being followed. To prevent Batses disappearing the police arrested him on October 23rd.

Batses at first denied all knowledge of smuggled money. Then he claimed that what he had received was simply contributions from foreign scientific associations for his monthly magazine *Antaios* (which had actually ceased publication that same month). Finally he made some vague allusions to one of his contact-men who, he said, may have been in contact with Ploumbides. The police made some more arrests.

★   ★   ★

But the Vavoudes Group itself was still intact. As a precaution, however, Vavoudes temporarily closed down the Villa Avra station and moved to the greater safety of the crypt at Lycurgus Street. From there, he informed Bucharest of what had happened. His masters took little time in suggesting arrangements for reestablishing contact between the Athens group and the sources of their money in France. Four days after Batses' arrest they wirelessed:

26K. Herewith yafka for Paris (yafka is the Russian word used by Greek Communists to describe a secret meeting-place) *begins: Madame Marcelle Bourgine, 168 Rue Lafayette, Paris. It is a post office. To enter and ask for Madame Bourgine. To say to her: Jean vous prie de lui donner un appareil photographique and to show it to her in writing. She will answer: Mais je n'ai plus un appareil Leica. The office is open from 8 to 12 and from 8* [sic] *to 6 on working days. If she herself is not there when our man goes, he must go again the next day. This yafka will operate from November.*

The passwords, which were given in Greek characters, were then repeated in French in a second message. Five days later on November 1st, a further message said:

After your man who goes to Paris for money has made the first contact with the yafka according to our signal 26 . . . he will give the second man from whom he will collect the money the code words . . . we have arranged.

For twenty-one days after Batses' arrest, the Vavoudes Group continued to function undisturbed. But meanwhile the police and security men were at last closing in. Their activities, however, were still quite unconnected with the Batses case.

* * *

For several years, they had been puzzled by the speed with which *Radio Free Greece* at Bucharest was broad-

casting news and comments about events in Athens. On
January 5th, 1950, a particularly curious case came to
their notice. The Greek Government had just resigned.
A special aircraft was sent from Athens to fetch a new
Prime Minister from Corfu. Only the King, a few senior
officials and some of the staff of Athens airport (which
happens to be not far from the Villa Avra) knew of the
departure. Just one hour later, while the aircraft was
still in flight, the news was broadcast by *Radio Free
Greece*.

Then, in June 1950, Greek army wireless technicians
picked up unregistered transmitters in the Athens area.
They were monitored and were found to be working
regular schedules with a distant station. Radiolocators
placed that station at or near Bucharest. Radiolocation
cars and a unit of the Greek fleet were called in to pin-
point the transmitters. Meanwhile, the messages, coded
in a five-figure cipher, were regularly monitored and
filed. But decoding experts failed to break the cipher
and the files grew fat with unintelligible messages.

For seventeen months, the radiolocation men strug-
gled with the problem of fixing the exact spot from
which the messages were being sent. Their task was
complicated by the fact that sometimes Lycurgus Street
and sometimes the Villa Avra were on the air, but rarely
both together. In the autumn of 1951, however, they
reported that they were nearing their two targets. The
Villa Avra station was working at the time, signalling
regularly every morning. As it stood a little apart from
neighboring buildings, it was easier to locate exactly
than the small terrace house in Lycurgus Street. In fact,
at Lycurgus Street, the experts suspected first number
43, then number 37, the home of an old communist
goldsmith named Toutoumis.

After long and careful checking, intelligence and

police officers agreed that the time had come to strike. They decided to raid both stations simultaneously and to choose a time when the Villa Avra was actually transmitting.

But at this point their plans were interrupted when the Villa station suddenly closed down. (This, though they did not know it, was a result of the arrest of Batses.) Then the radiolocation men reported that Lycurgus Street was now coming on the air with regular schedules shortly after midnight. The police changed their plans to fit this new situation.

In the early hours of the morning of November 14th, the Minister of the Interior, who had spent the night in his office, gave the signal. Strong detachments of police and security men surrounded the Villa Avra and a whole block of houses in Lycurgus Street. At the Villa everything went smoothly. Police entered quietly by the front door, using a skeleton key. Arghyriades' mistress was found in bed with the children and at first said that Arghyriades was away at his chicken farm. But she soon betrayed the entrance to the secret cellars. Inside Arghyriades was asleep. One of the transmitters was found there, together with code books, documents, paper, the printing press and some money. The second transmitter was later found at the chicken farm.

Meanwhile, at Lycurgus Street, Vavoudes was busy sending the night's messages from his crypt. But, as he tapped out the morse on his transmitter key each signal was making a needle jump more and more violently on a portable detector carried by a policeman who was moving closer along the dark, deserted street behind the house. He stopped behind number 37, convinced that he was within forty yards at most of the mysterious operator. Then the police trucks arrived and, as the policemen piled out and surrounded the block, Vavou-

des abruptly broke off in the middle of a group of
letters and switched out the lights in his crypt.

At number 37 the goldsmith and his son were questioned and their house searched, but the police found
nothing. At number 39, the Caloumenos family boldly
denied all knowledge of transmitters and secret hide-
outs. "Tear my house down brick by brick," said the
old carpenter defiantly, "you will find nothing here."
His wife and children too, closely questioned, refused
stubbornly to talk.

For the next thirty-six hours, policemen, soldiers and
communications experts searched every nook and cran-
ny in the house. They tapped walls, lifted floor-boards,
drilled holes in ceilings. They found a number of minor
hiding-places used for messages, a concealed cupboard
behind a wall, but still no sign of the main crypt. A
mine-detection squad was sent for next and swept the
yard behind the house. Metal was located at a point
some distance from the back entrance. A shaft was sunk
there but revealed only some iron piping leading to a
cesspit. Again the mine detector swept the yard. This
time persistent signals came from a spot immediately
below the kitchen steps. Vigorous efforts were made to
shift the steps but they would not move. But now, beside the steps, a small piece of mortar was dislodged.
It revealed a round hole, about the size of a golf ball,
leading to a dark, hollow space. In his excitement, the
officer in charge shouted, "Come out of there, we've
found you." To his amazement his bluff worked. A
muffled voice replied from the dark, "I won't come out.
I'm armed with three revolvers and plenty of ammunition. If anyone comes near, I'll shoot." It was the voice
of Nicholas Vavoudes.

For three more hours, police and army officers tried
every way of coaxing Vavoudes to surrender, mean-

while desperately searching for a way to open up the crypt without precipitating his suicide. The Minister of the Interior himself was sent for, and arrived with a squad of Greek and foreign journalists who watched what followed. The Minister promised Vavoudes he would be well treated after his arrest. But when Vavoudes demanded an assurance that his life would, in all circumstances, be spared, the Minister could only answer, "That will depend on you."

Finally, Vavoudes asked for a few more moments to think things over. His request was granted and the police again halted their efforts to force an entrance. There was a short silence inside the crypt. Then a small wisp of smoke curled from a chimney above the kitchen roof. Vavoudes had started to burn incriminating papers. A policeman dashed to pour water down the chimney. The smoke died out. Then, there were two sharp reports and silence.

★   ★   ★

Three months later the trial opened before the Athens Permanent Court Martial. The only charge was military espionage. The big, dingy courtroom on Venizelos Street was packed with spectators, journalists, lawyers and police. On eight rows of benches in the center, facing the five judges, sat twenty-nine prisoners. The thirtieth was absent. Vavoudes had died, without regaining consciousness, soon after he was lifted from the crypt. His place as chief defendant was taken by Nicholas Belogiannes, the Central Committee member who had once given Vavoudes orders. It was a role which Belogiannes well understood. Already sentenced to death after his arrest in 1950, his execution had been indefinitely postponed. Now, with the eyes of a new Court on him, he determined to maintain his revolu-

tionary record. He sat laughing and joking with his
companions, reading newspapers or a slim book of
English lyric poems or sniffing a red carnation, apparently indifferent to the proceedings. Then, when his
turn came to speak, he lectured the judges on communist policy and bluntly denied that communists were
spies.

"The evidence produced about the Communist Party's
illegal apparatus," he said, "is nobody's secret. It is a
principle of the party since 1903 when Lenin first for-
mulated it and spoke of the combination of legal and
illegal work. The illegal apparatus is a matter of legiti-
mate defense. . . .

"A new war must not find Greece against the Soviet
Union. In following this policy, we watch all aspects of
public life in Greece. All its aspects interest us: political,
social and naturally whatever may concern the military
preparation of the country. . . .

"This trial will show that communism has indestruct-
ible roots in Greece, watered by blood it has shed for
the Greek people."

His former mistress, Elli Ioannides, followed his example on the witness stand, flatly rejecting all charges,
refusing to answer questions and expounding her party's
line. And, in her last statement, she demanded that if
the Court sentenced her to death then, like others, she
should be shot. The fact that she was a woman was
irrelevant, she said, and she did not ask for mercy.

In his turn, young Lazarides, Vavoudes' second assistant at the Villa Avra (whose sister had escaped arrest) was equally defiant. "I never thought of betraying
the man who was like a father to me," he said of Zachariades, his party's leader. "Besides I believe in the communist ideology."

But others told a different story. Pleading that he

had never known the real purpose of Vavoudes' work, the lawyer Batses begged for forgiveness, insisted that he had helped the police in their investigations, and offered to volunteer for immediate service at the Korean front.

Arghyriades, Vavoudes' assistant at the Villa Avra, also pleaded ignorance of the network's purpose. "I knew nothing about spying," he said. "I knew only that we were in contact with the Politbureau." And he added, "I wanted to be a simple party member, not to get mixed up in work like that." But he feared to leave when Vavoudes threatened him, he claimed. "He even made me weep," he said.

A similar story was told by Caloumenos, the old carpenter of Lycurgus Street. "I was terrorized by Vavoudes. He threatened he would kill us all. . . . He was the master in my house. . . . Even at the last moment I was afraid that he would kill my children." And the eldest of the children, Margaret, added her account of the fear inspired by their "satanic" guest.

Of the twenty-nine defendants, twenty-one claimed that they were neither communists nor spies but had been used as mere catspaws. Four others said they had not understood the implications of their work and asked the Court for mercy. The remaining four defiantly defended the Communist Party and all its actions. But though their reactions were so varied, not one of the prisoners questioned the main facts on which the case was based. Those facts had been established partly during interrogations of the prisoners themselves, but mostly from a mass of documentary evidence discovered in the raids on the transmitter stations.

At the Villa Avra and Lycurgus Street, five code books were found undamaged. Vavoudes himself had not dared to start burning his papers at the beginning of the raid, for fear of revealing where he was hidden to the searchers. If he had, he would soon have been stifled in his airless crypt. Only after he had decided to shoot himself did he begin gropingly to set light to whatever he could lay his hands on. By then it was too late.

With the help of the captured papers, experts were now able to decipher all the messages monitored since 1950. Others were found unciphered in Vavoudes' crypt. Altogether, over 300 messages were published; a few more were withheld, on security grounds, by the Greek Government.

Later, *Radio Free Greece* and communists elsewhere denounced the messages as forgeries and the trial as a "fascist provocation" and added, incidentally, that Arghyriades was a police agent. But neither the defendants themselves, who spoke with the greatest freedom throughout the trial ("I am not terrorized and I cannot say that terrorism has been used against me," said Belogiannes), nor their lawyers made any such claims. In court, the validity of no single message was ever challenged.

★   ★   ★

By the morning of March 1st, the Court's work was done. The prisoners made their final statements and were taken away under heavy escort. Then the courtroom was cleared and the judges withdrew. Four hours later, the President, Colonel John Simos, led his colleagues back on to the raised wooden dais. A squad of gendarmes presented arms. Spectators and lawyers stood as the Colonel read out the verdict. But the prisoners were absent. By Greek custom, they would hear their sentences later in their cells. Eight were condemned to death, including Nicholas Belogiannes, his mistress, Elli Ioannides, Elias Arghyriades of the Villa Avra, the carpenter Caloumenos and the lawyer Batses. Four received life sentences. Ten got prison terms of from one to twenty years. The remaining seven were freed.

The prisoners sentenced to death appealed for a reprieve to the Council of Pardons, and it was then that a strange thing happened. Nicholas Ploumbides, the Central Committee member who had organized EDA for the elections, was still at large. He had made a narrow escape when he left the house of one of Batses' financial contact-men the day before that man and his wife was arrested. Now, from his new hiding-place, he wrote a letter to the two defense counsel of Belogiannes and sent copies to all the Athens newspapers and to the correspondents of *Reuters* and *Tass*. In it he claimed that the trial had been staged by the Greek General Staff at the insistence of the Americans, that Belogiannes was being tried for his political convictions, and that evidence that he was in charge of the Communist Party's illegal apparatus had been faked. He wrote:

I declare:

(1) that the chief of the illegal apparatus of the Greek Communist Party was myself and not Belogiannes. For this function and for my actions I accept all responsibilities. After this declaration of mine, every insistence on the execution of Belogiannes is unjustified, unjust and a clearly murderous act.

(2) that it may not be supposed that I am acting the hero from a position of safety I promise to surrender to the authorities and stand trial if the death sentences on my friend and comrade N. Belogiannes are changed.

Use this letter wherever you think fit (Council of Pardons, Press, etc.).

Yours truly,
N. PLOUMBIDES,
Member of the C.C. of the C.P.G.

P.S. To authenticate my signature, apart from my handwriting, which is known to many, I also give my finger print.

But it seems that Ploumbides was acting without his party leaders. Immediately the letter was published, *Radio Free Greece* at once denied its authenticity, claimed that it was forged by the police and announced that Ploumbides himself was in a sanatorium for tuberculosis behind the Iron Curtain.

*   *   *

The story of the Vavoudes Group ended on March 30th. Four of the death sentences had been commuted to life imprisonment. The other four were carried out. In the light of headlamps from nearby army lorries Nicholas Belogiannes, Demetrius Batses, Elias Arghyriades and Nicholas Caloumenos were shot at dawn.

There was one curious sequel eight months later. At about midnight on November 25th, Nicholas Ploumbides went home to the little corner house at number 14 Preveza Street where he was then in hiding. He changed into a pair of silk pyjamas, and sat down for a late meal. He was still at the table when two police officers came in and told him that he was under arrest. Impassive, he claimed that there was some mistake. He was George Panopoulos, a merchant, he said, and showed them an identity card in that name, issued in 1945. But one of the policemen knew him well. "You've beaten me," Ploumbides admitted, and was led quietly away to police headquarters.

Two days later *Radio Free Greece* broadcast an official statement by the Central Committee of the Greek Communist Party. Of the man who had been a party member for a quarter of a century, had served in its Politbureau from 1937, had officially represented it at meetings of the Cominform in Moscow, had been one of its Members of Parliament, had suffered imprisonment and exile on its behalf, had lived in constant danger in Athens for the past seven years to do its work, whose health was ruined, whose wife was in jail, whose sister had been shot and whose child was in an orphanage—of Nicholas Ploumbides, the Central Committee now had this to say:

The C.C. of the C.P.G. announces that N. Ploumbides, alias Barbas, has for twenty-seven years been an agent of the Security Police in the ranks of the C.P.G. . . . among his biggest betrayals is that he betrayed to the Security Police and to the scaffold the peoples' hero N. Belogiannes . . .

The C.C. of the C.P.G. today unmasks the provocateur Ploumbides, alias Barbas. All the concrete facts concerning the police spying activity of Ploumbides will be published at the suitable time. . . .

What was the real motive for this strange denunciation? Ploumbides himself was tried, sentenced as a spy, and executed in 1954. But the Cental Committee's "facts" are still unpublished.

★

The Swedish Traitors

★

"There is nothing, sir," Doctor Johnson once asserted, "that you may not muster up some plausible arguments for." No doubt an able communist propagandist, discussing (if he were allowed to) the stories of Dr. Sorge, Colonel Zabotin and Nicholas Vavoudes, could muster up some such arguments to show how the circumstances of each of these cases justified the actions of the Russians and their spies. Japan, he might say, was an enemy; so Sorge's work was merely self-defense. Canada was a great Power which might one day join an alliance against Russia; so it was self-defense again. And Greece was in the throes of civil war; so ordinary standards do not apply.

But even the ablest communist propagandist would find it hard to muster up an argument for Ernst Hilding Andersson or Fritiof Enbom.

The last two cases in this book took place in Sweden: a traditionally neutral, small country, obviously threatening no one, with a society as prosperous and stable as any in the world. In fact, it is hard to understand how communists can exist at all in Sweden—let alone communist spies for Russia. But they do: some 20,000 party members and perhaps a few hundred actual or potential spies.

As a political force, the Swedish Communist Party is negligible. It now wins not more than four votes out of every hundred at elections. But as a fifth column it could be, and has been, a serious menace—as the Andersson and Enbom cases show.

183

It is Sweden's misfortune—but evidently no accident—that most of her communists are concentrated in the extreme north: precisely the area which would be most vulnerable to attack from Russia. Experts disagree over the reason for this fact: it is tradition, they say, or the climate, or the remoteness, or the proximity of Finnish communists across the border. Certainly it is no longer because work is short and wages low; though they have been in the past.

At all events, the Communist Party is three times stronger in northern Sweden than in the south. All the Swedish spies whose stories are told in the next three chapters were communists, except one. Many of them were northerners, and most of their spying concerned Swedish military defenses in the north.

The information which they stole could have been of value to the Russians only on one assumption: that Russia was planning to invade Sweden. The spies themselves believed that that was Russia's plan.

The Swedish public—except the communists—were profoundly shocked by the Andersson and Enbom cases. They suddenly saw what they had not believed before: that communist subversion, and such things as Russian-sponsored spies, were not reserved exclusively for a cold war between big Powers. Andersson and Enbom killed the comfortable theory that "it can't happen here." Perhaps that was just as well.

XIII

The Successful Sailor

★

Ernst Hilding Andersson was a successful sailor. He thought so himself, and his colleagues and superiors agreed. His career in the Royal Swedish Navy could hardly have been better. In twenty-four years of service, he had never once had an adverse report. He had done exceptionally well in the many specialist courses he had taken, and had risen from Stoker to Engineer Warrant Officer. He was no leader, perhaps, and he had few close personal friends among his shipmates; but they all respected him as an intelligent, hard-working and thoroughly reliable man.

He was dark, of medium height and sturdily built, and—like many of his countrymen—a person of few words. In the navy, he spoke little of his early life or of the disadvantages he had successfully overcome. But he was certainly not a man with a personal grievance; though he did, perhaps, believe that he was capable of higher things than he had yet achieved.

His parents had been tobacco workers until a government monopoly took over the industry, when they retired on a small pension to a little farm at Strängnäs about sixty miles from Stockholm. Andersson's father was rheumatic and, with a wife and eight children to keep, found it hard to make ends meet. He was a gifted and intelligent person, but Andersson did not get on with him, and his childhood was lonely and unhappy. One sister died of tuberculosis and another was taken away to a mental home. At school Andersson did well, but had to leave when he was only twelve. For three years, he worked for neighboring farmers, at low wages for long hours. Then, when he was sixteen, he decided to leave home. For a year he stayed with one of his sisters in Stockholm and worked as an errand boy. In the autumn of 1927, he volunteered and joined the navy. Three years later he met his wife, and they were married in 1933 when he was twenty-four. She was a simple woman, very much his inferior intellectually and often unable to understand him. But she found him "kind, considerate and good," not frivolous and not an excessive drinker. Their son was born in 1949.

Apart from his naval career, Andersson had many intellectual interests. He wanted to make up for his inadequate education, read widely and studied an extraordinary variety of subjects: science, philosophy, astronomy, mathematics, English, German and Russian. In 1945, he completed in three terms an advanced course on electricity at a Stockholm technical advanced school, which should have taken eight. To his young nephew, "Uncle Ernst" was something of a hero, and he was a devoted father to his own small son. His shipmates elected him to the Executive Committees of the Petty Officers' and Naval Engineers' Associations.

In fact, until September 21st, 1951, there seemed to have been nothing at all remarkable about the story of Warrant Officer Andersson of the Royal Swedish Navy except, perhaps, his professional success. A dull man, one might have said, with a dull but satisfactory adult life.

But on that day Andersson was arrested as a Soviet

spy: "the most dangerous spy exposed in Sweden" according to the Chief of the Swedish General Staff.

★   ★   ★

The investigations which followed uncovered a story which caused a sensation in Sweden, both because of the damage he had done to the security of that country and also because of the apparent ease with which he had worked. The story is also of interest for a third reason: because, to everyone but himself, his motives —remote, abstract, theoretical motives—seemed so completely irrelevant to the actions which they made him take.

After Andersson was caught, it was discovered that he had had connections with the Swedish Communist Party for many years. A local clergyman said that his parents, too, though politically inactive, had been well-known communist sympathizers.

Soon after Andersson joined the navy, he was taken by a colleague to a meeting and "social" organized by the Communist Party in Stockholm. Still lonely and rather ill at ease, he liked the friendly atmosphere and became interested. He began to read communist books and, a year later, joined the Young Communist League. In 1929, he started to write unsigned articles for an illegal publication, the *Torpedo*, which the Communist Party used for making anti-militarist propaganda among the sailors. He was also responsible for distributing copies of the *Torpedo* and for recruiting sailors in the navy into the Young Communist League.

It was at this time that he first met Sixten Rogeby, the man who later introduced him to his Russian spymasters. Rogeby had joined the navy in 1929 and was associated with the *Torpedo*. He left the service in 1931 and took part in the Spanish civil war. Andersson met him again after his return to Sweden, and was impressed by his militancy and the stories he told of his experiences abroad. During the second world war, Rogeby was called up for further naval service, but was discharged as "unsuitable" in 1943. He then joined the staff of the Swedish Communist Party's official daily newspaper *Ny Dag*, and in 1949 was sent as its correspondent to Moscow where he stayed for nearly two years. It was suggested that Rogeby underwent special training while he was in the Soviet Union.

Meanwhile, in the late autumn of 1946, Andersson visited Rogeby's home. There he met the First Secretary to the Soviet Legation in Stockholm, Constantine Vinogradov. They had a long, serious talk and left Rogeby's home together. Vinogradov was impressed and invited Andersson to dinner at his flat. There was a lavish meal which included caviar, and Andersson drank seven or eight glasses of schnapps (the Russian drank fewer, saying that he had a weak heart). Then they settled down to a long discussion over coffee, liqueurs and, later, grog. They talked for five or six hours; first about politics and general matters, then about conditions at the Stockholm naval dockyard where Andersson was then serving. By the end of the evening, Andersson had clearly understood what it was the Russian wanted—and he knew that the Russian realized that he had understood.

On New Year's Eve, Vinogradov called at Andersson's home with a present of four bottles of spirits. He again invited the Warrant Officer to his flat and there introduced him to Victor Pavlovich Anissimov, the young Stockholm correspondent of the *Tass* news agency. Andersson did not meet Vinogradov again: the First Secretary had done his work. But, from then on, he saw a great deal of Anissimov. They went for long bicycle rides and picnics together, and, over the picnic meals which the Russian provided, Andersson told Anissimov his life story in great detail, showed him various naval certificates and testimonials and posed for a series of portrait photographs taken from various angles. Then, when these preliminaries were completed, Anissimov explained that, in future, it would be unwise for them to be seen together, or for Andersson to visit his flat at Brantingsgatan. They therefore agreed on a number of secret meeting-places outside Stockholm.

*   *   *

At the end of November 1949, Andersson was given his first specific spying task: just three years after he had first been sounded by Vinogradov. Anissimov asked him to produce detailed answers to three questions: what warships were stationed at the Stockholm naval base and what was their state of readiness; what were the expected future movements of these ships and what plans were there for refitting them; and what were the composition and disposition of the coastal fleet operating in the Baltic?

Anissimov had given Andersson no guidance about how to find this information: he was entirely dependent on himself. Some of the answers he already knew; for the rest he relied on discreet questioning of naval colleagues, sometimes deliberately making inaccurate statements which, in view of his reputation and seniority, they were often delighted to be able to correct. He took two weeks to prepare his report, and had some difficulty with answering the questions about the coastal fleet. Anissimov criticized him for omitting information about minesweepers, and Andersson wrote him a further report, which he passed to him in December 1949.

At about this time he received his first payment from the Russians. It came in the shape of a "loan" of 500 Swedish crowns (about $75) shortly before his son was born, followed by a "gift" of a further 500 to Mrs. Andersson and the baby. From then on, Andersson was expected to supply continuous reports on the Stockholm naval station.

He met Anissimov again on May 27th, handed in a further report (in invisible ink) and was given 400 crowns and his instructions for his next assignment written on a small slip of paper. He was to make a detailed report on defense measures at the Skeppsholmen base in Stockholm, together with a sketch map of the area. With his usual care and accuracy, Andersson bought a published map of the district and from it made a greatly enlarged map of the base. On this he marked and numbered every building, office, depot, shelter and shed. He noted where each senior officer worked, the number of entrances to each shelter, and the thickness of its walls and doors.

Meanwhile he learned that he had been appointed to the naval icebreaker, *Ymer*, which was due to leave for an overhaul at Karlskrona, the big naval base and dockyard on the south coast of Sweden, on June 10th. Anissimov promptly asked for a similar report on this area as well, together with a description of the ships there and of the surrounding fortifications. Once again, Andersson compiled a detailed map (copying one which he borrowed from the dockyard electrical workshop), on which he marked 800 items of interest including all buildings and the position of anti-aircraft artillery, machine-gun nests and ammunition sheds. Some of his observations he made while ostensibly picking mushrooms on the islands near the base (an activity for which, incidentally, two Russians were arrested that year near a military airfield, which was out of bounds to foreigners, at Järva.) He also added notes on the local coastal artillery regiment, on the civilian employees at the dockyard, and on some British naval vessels which happened to be visiting Karlskrona, one of which he boarded. He reported that he had asked the British sailors their views on the world situation and what they thought of the Russians, whether they expected another war and what they were doing in the Baltic. From their replies, he claimed to have drawn conclusions (though what those conclusions were is not recorded) on the morale of the Royal Navy. Until his return to Stockholm, Andersson tried to keep most of his observations in his head—he had an excellent memory—but he also hid four pages of notes in a pair of boots.

He returned to Stockholm and met Anissimov at Orby, on the outskirts of the capital, late in September. At this meeting he emphasized the risks that he had been taking, but the Russian merely answered that they "were necessary for the cause." Soon afterwards they met again at a picnic at Stäket, to the north-west of Stockholm, where the Russian showed him how to use his camera and gave him 1,200 crowns in order to buy himself a similar machine. Then, on December 6th, Andersson called at Anissimov's flat (one of the rare occasions when he did so) with a final report on the current situation at the Stockholm base, a few hours before sailing north with his ship. He received instructions for that journey, and arranged to meet the Russian again in the coming summer on June 4th.

★   ★   ★

His new assignment was the most important he had yet undertaken. He was asked to give details of fortifications and defense works along the north-eastern Swedish coast, and to report on harbors and on areas suitable for landings: places which it would be important for the Russians to occupy "before"—as Anissimov put it—"the Americans dropped tens of thousands of men there." The coastal defenses were very highly secret. Some of them were new and the approaches to them were often closed to all but Swedish naval craft, so that only a member of the Swedish navy would have the opportunity to observe them closely.

Andersson made careful preparations for his voyage on the icebreaker. For his camera he bought a number of rolls of film, an expensive light-meter, three filters, a telephoto lens, a flash attachment, developing equipment and a photographic handbook. He fitted up a dark room on board ship and told his shipmates that his interest in amateur photography had come after a lucky win in the football pools.

For the next six months, he lost no opportunity of noting information useful to the Russians and of photographing, whenever he could, defense installations and other points of interest along the coast. The *Ymer* sailed first to Luleå in northern Sweden where Andersson studied new fortification works in the area, then down to a naval depot at Gustavsvik where he photographed the docks and workshops. On March 31st, his ship bunkered at a fuelling station in the Stockholm archipelago, where he took a series of pictures of entrances and tunnels to underground stores and defense works, and then sailed north again to Luleå where she stayed for two weeks. At a party given by non-commissioned officers of the Air Force, he learned details of the 21st Wing based ner Luleå, and on May 16th was invited with his colleagues to visit the fortress of Boden, headquarters of the northern military command and the central point of north Sweden's defensive system. Here, in a ring of mountains, are atom-bomb-proof storehouses and galleries in which a man can travel for 50 miles underground. Guides explained that what they were about to see was secret, and the visitors were asked to surrender cameras; but Andersson contrived to memorize, and later note, descriptions of a power-house, fire-control centers, the location and caliber of guns, the layout of magazines and defense works and many other details. Gunnery courses which he had taken helped him in his observations.

On May 18th, the *Ymer* returned to Stockholm. Andersson prepared a detailed, twelve-page report with many photographs and maps attached. He also sent a few, innocent photographs which he had taken during the voyage to an official naval magazine, where they were later published. But for some reason, he failed to keep the appointment with the Russian which he had previously made for June 4th. During his absence, however, Victor Anissimov had left Stockholm. He had returned to Moscow on April 20th where, it was reported, he had joined the staff of Lavrenti Beria, then still head of the N.K.V.D. His place as Andersson's contact-man had been taken by a certain Nicholas Petrovich Orlov whose official status was chauffeur to the Russian Naval Attaché, Presnakov.

On June 5th—the day after his appointment—an unknown "friend" telephoned to Andersson, arranged to meet him on the 6th in a Stockholm street, and explained the following recognition signals. Andersson was to carry a suitcase with a roll of paper protruding from it. On seeing him, Orlov was to ask, "Does bus 42 run this way?" Andersson: "No, only bus 55." Orlov:

"How's Ester?" Andersson: "She's at Malmö for the moment." They duly met. Andersson handed over his report and was paid 700 crowns.

At about this time, the Warrant Officer was appointed to the destroyer *Öland*. Then he was offered a position as an engineer at the Stockholm naval yard which would have meant a higher rate of pay. He discussed the matter with Orlov, who advised him to refuse and offered to compensate him for his financial loss. Instead Andersson joined a radar course, and a few days later Orlov sent him 230 crowns.

★   ★   ★

Then came the last assignment. On the evening of September 11th, the Soviet "chauffeur," Orlov, cycled across Stockholm to the trolley viaduct at Tegelbacken near the central railway station. There, by a corner of a lemonade kiosk under the viaduct, he parked his machine in a bicycle stand and walked away. Next day, Andersson also cycled round to Tegelbacken. He left his own bicycle in the same stand, mounted Orlov's and rode off to the hospital on the southern outskirts of the city. There he parked Orlov's cycle near the main entrance, opened the tool box and took out a roll of two sheets of paper, tied with a blue and yellow ribbon (the Swedish national colors), which he put in his pocket. He then took a trolley home. The papers contained instructions and, inside them, he found 1,200 crowns in 100-crown notes.

The following morning, September 13th, Andersson went to the naval station and asked for five days' leave to attend to urgent family business at Nässjö in Central Sweden. He then went straight to the Central Station and took a direct train south to Karlskrona where he arrived that evening. He spent the next day in the naval yard having a general look round, and confirmed that, as Orlov had told him, seven British naval vessels were visiting the base: the destroyer *Zambesi*, a depot ship *Montclare*, a tender and four submarines. The following morning, a Saturday, he went to the quay where *Zambesi* was moored and spoke to several of the crew. That afternoon, he changed into civilian clothes and joined the crowd of visitors to *Montclare*. By saying that he had been specially invited by a friend, he managed to get access to parts of the ship which were not open to the public. He then went ashore where he struck up an acquaintance with one of *Zambesi's* engineers who later showed him round the destroyer. On the evening of Sunday the 16th, he returned to Stockholm and was back on duty at the naval station on Monday.

On the morning of Thursday, September 20th, Orlov again parked his bicycle (which he had meanwhile fetched from the hospital) under the viaduct at Tegelbacken. That afternoon, after he had finished work, Andersson collected it and once more rode to the hospital building. He took from his briefcase a sheaf of eight sheets of paper covered with invisible writing, wrapped them round the bicycle pump and put them into the tool box. He then again went home by trolleycar.

But by now, Andersson had been under observation for some time. He was arrested on his way to work next morning and taken to the headquarters of the Stockholm Criminal Police.

For five days, he persisted in denying all knowledge of espionage or Russians. Then, confronted with documentary evidence which included his last report on Karlskrona, he confessed.

His confessions added little to what the police already suspected, but they were useful as confirmation. It appeared that he had had no idea that he was watched, was surprised by his arrest and had prepared no defense or alibi of any kind. But he showed little emotion. Though he was slightly concerned about the effects on his son's education, he was fatalistic about his own future and regretted only that he would now be prevented from doing still more important spying. He seemed a little resentful that his talents had been wasted on simple assignments and that he would not be able to serve the Russians in the war which he apparently believed was coming, when he might, he thought, have done something really big.

*   *   *

On October 6th, the trial opened in public in a Stockholm magistrate's court packed with spectators, journalists and with diplomats from twenty countries. But apparently there was no Russian present. (Orlov, incidentally, had meanwhile been expelled from Sweden.) Andersson's wife declined to testify. Later, the proceedings were held *in camera*, and part of the evidence, giving details of military information he had stolen, was not published. Andersson made it clear that he fully understood the implications and probable consequences of what he had done. He sat motionless at attention listening to the prosecutor's case, and answered questions, looking straight at his questioner, briefly but directly without either irrelevancies or boasting. On only three occasions did he show any concern: once when he was asked to leave the court while his former friend Sixten Rogeby gave evidence, once when he expressed regret that he had not destroyed some notes which the police had found, and once when the prosecutor reminded him that he had admitted to the police having been a member of the Young Communist League. This he now denied, adding, "It is impossible for me to know whether or not I was enrolled. I got a badge, but that does not mean membership. I never paid a subscription and never held a card."

But though, in court, he denied membership, he made it perfectly clear that it was his communist views and his association with the Communist Party which had led him to become a spy.

"I have held certain views about political and economic events in the world, for twenty years," he said. "If one meets people with the same interests, it is natural that one should collaborate. In all circumstances I intended to give what help I could. . . . My political outlook is clear. Of course I had some qualms but I repressed them." And he added: "I was working for what I consider right and just and I felt independent of what other people thought. In so far as our collaboration would lead sooner or later to the goal, I was ready to do my share. I was fully aware of the consequences my work could have for myself, my country and humanity. My qualms were caused by the thought that I might not be sufficiently effective."

When he was asked whether, if a war had broken out while he was still serving in the navy, he would have continued to pass information, he answered: "My conviction would not be changed if Sweden were involved in a war against the Soviet Union. It would only be more firmly rooted. In any given situation, I would regard the British and Americans as my enemies." When asked about his decision to start spying, he said: "I would not like to say that I made a decision; but rather that I have found no reasons not to act as I have done."

Andersson pleaded guilty, and was sentenced to imprisonment for life with hard labor—the maximum sentence—for "gross military, naval and economic espionage for a foreign power, and gross neglect of his duty as a Warrant Officer of the Royal Swedish Navy, and illegal intelligence against a foreign power" (Great Britain). He did not appeal.

Meanwhile, the Communist Party and its newspapers declared that Andersson had never been a communist, and denounced the whole affair as "provocation." "The Communist Party," wrote *Ny Dag* on November 3rd, "accepts just as little as the rest of the Swedish people the deeds of which Andersson is guilty. Had he belonged to our party he would have been expelled." And, in a leading article on November 6th, *Ny Dag* added that the case could "only be accounted for if one assumes that Ernst Hilding Andersson is a provocateur, a tool in the hands of the forces which seek to involve Sweden in the war of aggression they have planned against the Soviet Union."

★   ★   ★

In a way, Andersson's case is the most puzzling of all the cases mentioned in this book. Not because the facts are in any way obscure: on the contrary the story of what he did and how he did it is clear, straightforward and well documented. Nor because his motive is in any doubt: Andersson was a convinced, ideological communist who firmly believed that to spy for Russia against his own country was a necessary contribution in a struggle for a worthy cause. What is so difficult to understand is how and why such a man as he could come to that conclusion.

For most of the other spies whose activities have been described, one can find some sort of acceptable, personal explanation. One can at least guess at the emotions, ideas and experiences which determined the way they acted. Sorge was himself half Russian, son of a ruined bourgeois family, who grew up at the front during the first world war, witnessed the collapse of the old society, threw himself into the communist movement when it first began, and then, still in the early days, went to work for the Comintern in Moscow. Rose and Carr, immigrants from Russia, "second class citizens," were perhaps already Soviet agents when they came to Canada. Nunn May, the earnest, ordinary little man, was suddenly burdened with the responsibility of great secrets which he had neither the character nor the training to bear. Vavoudes, Belogiannes, and some of their Greek comrades were men who had suffered in the past and who found themselves caught up in an attempted revolution in a country beset by social and economic problems. For all these men, one can find explanations and excuses. But not for Ernst Hilding Andersson.

His childhood, it is true, had been hard and lonely. His marriage was not a great success. But many men have suffered worse handicaps without becoming revolutionaries or spies. Besides he had triumphantly overcome his early difficulties. He had done as well as, perhaps better than, any man in his situation could have hoped, and he admitted as much himself. The personal motive, therefore, is difficult to find.

But certainly there are men who, though they have no personal sense of grievance, become communists or fanatics because they are disgusted by injustices to others or the sufferings of their fellows. Often these men make the most powerful revolutionaries of all. But here again, in the case of Andersson, the explanation seems to fail.

"Sweden," he himself said, "is a prosperous country and the capitalist system seems to suit the Swedes well. The standard of living is higher than in other countries.

"But," he added, "we cannot judge by existing conditions. We have to work on a long-term basis. . . . My decision to work for the Soviet Union matured along with my conviction. It was the logical conclusion."

So it seems that "logic" is the answer: a logic so abstract, so theoretical, so remote from reality, that it made all actual facts and situations—the welfare of his family, his personal success, the prosperity and safety of his countrymen—irrelevant and unimportant.

If there were any personal subjective influences at work as well, then the most important of them were probably the deep impression made on him by his reading of Marx, Lenin and Stalin, soon after he joined the navy; the comradeship he found among the communists in the early days of his association with them; and also, perhaps, his over-estimation of his own ability and intelligence. For though he was, in fact, both able and intelligent, he was essentially an ordinary man. But he believed himself to be capable of bigger things than service as a Warrant Officer in the Swedish Navy.

But how does this analysis fit with the fact that Andersson took money? Altogether he is known to have received nearly 5,000 crowns ($750). He did not deny that he was paid, but claimed that he had spent more than he received, and very probably this was so. Certainly he had no personal financial worries. Money was not a motive or any part of the reason why he spied.

The explanation seems to be this. For the Russians (for reasons discussed elsewhere) it is the established practice to pay spies—whether they want payment or resent it. This being so, Andersson saw no reason to refuse. The Russians gave him money, he took it and he signed receipts. The whole matter was a completely unimportant detail—as unimportant as the opinions of other people, or the fact that after his arrest his former comrades denounced him as a provocateur.

Andersson is now in jail in Sweden, his case a *cause célèbre*. But almost all the people who knew him best still find it hard to understand just *why* Andersson became a Soviet spy.

XIV

The Spy Who Cracked

★

Jan Lodin was a student at Stockholm University. He was a member of the Young Communist League and of a communist-inspired organization called *Clarté* which does propaganda among intellectuals. Certainly, by any definition, he was an intellectual himself: a small, fair-haired, rather intense young man who took a great interest in people and claimed to be something of an amateur psychologist. He was married to a girl who was a communist, like himself, and they lived together in a small flat in a suburb to the south of Stockholm.

Jan Lodin appears briefly in this story about spies, because it was he who first exposed the second big, post-war, Swedish spy case.

It all started, as far as Lodin was concerned, one evening in the summer of 1950. He had gone to a meeting held by *Clarté* at the University. When the speeches were over, he was introduced to an acquaintance of his wife, a twenty-nine-year-old communist called Lilian Ceder. They danced together and drank tea, and Lilian Ceder told him that she had recently come south from Luleå in northern Sweden where she had been on the staff of the local communist newspaper (the oldest communist daily in Sweden), the *Norrskensflamman*. Now, she said, she was working as a typist, and she also wrote occasional film reviews for the *Ny Dag*, the Stockholm communist daily. She was a tall, thin girl, unattractive physically and studious-looking. But Lodin thought her intelligent, though he later concluded that she was emotional and involved.

From then on, the Lodins saw a good deal of Lilian Ceder. Though Jan Lodin himself left the Communist Party in February 1951, she still came often to their home. One day, the following summer, she had a meal with them. They noticed that she was unusually excited and seemed very worried. And they were surprised and puzzled when, in a confused, nervous way, she began to hint that she had been involved in some kind of illegal work, that "a foreign embassy had a file" on her, and that she might be in danger of arrest. Meanwhile, she had also told the Lodins of her friendship, while she was in the north, with a fellow communist journalist on the staff of the *Norrskensflamman*. This man, who was separated from his wife, had now left Luleå and was working at a low-paid job at a Stockholm factory. He was in serious financial difficulty and, said Lilian Ceder, badly needed looking after. She asked the Lodins whether they could give him a room in their small flat. They agreed, and, in mid-October, the new lodger moved in.

★   ★   ★

Fritiof Enbom was a short man with thin, blond hair, a pale face and an untidy, bohemian appearance. He was clever, had an exceptional memory, and was an excellent talker. He shared with Lodin an interest in politics, literature and psychology, and said that he was writing an autobiographical novel. Despite his indifferent looks, he was, it seemed, very attractive to some women and had led a dissolute life. He had been a

communist for many years, but had lately become critical of his party.

As Lodin got to know Enbom better, he learned something of his early career. He was thirty-two years old
and had been born in a small remote village in the
forest some miles from the northern fortress city of
Boden. His father had had a small farm and had also
worked as a railway linesman, but had died in 1934.
There were four children—three boys and a girl—but
Enbom's elder brother had been taken to a mental
home. The family was left bankrupt at his father's
death, but his mother had just managed to save the
farm. They had lived in very poor conditions, and the
surviving boys had started work early, though Fritiof
(unlike his younger brother Martin) had been able to
attend the local secondary school. Then he had worked
for a year as a lumberjack before going south and becoming a gardener near Stockholm. Enbom had already joined the Young Communist League in northern
Sweden and now made contact with the party in the
capital. He became friendly with a prominent member,
Knut Olsson (later one of the editors of the *Ny Dag*)
who found him a job in a communist-sponsored organization called *Red Help* which was engaged in assisting refugees from Nazi Germany to come—sometimes
illegally—to Sweden.

In 1939 Enbom was called into the army and served
for a year in an artillery regiment at Boden. Then, in
March 1941, he became a railway linesman, like his
father before him, and worked for the next six years
at Boden and at a small station at Bjurå not far away.
In 1943 he married a local girl, and they had two children. But the marriage did not last. In May 1947, he
joined the staff of the *Norskensflamman* as its Boden

correspondent and later moved to the paper's head office at Luleå. In 1948, he met Lilian Ceder, who fell in love with him and with whom he was on intimate terms for some two years. In May 1951, he came south to Stockholm.

Lodin listened with interest to this story of Enbom. But he was still more interested in the man's strange state of mind. It soon became clear that, quite apart from his financial difficulties, Enbom was deeply worried. He was living a completely disorganized life, was sleeping badly and was neglecting his appearance even more than usual. He seemed to be hiding some curious secret. When talking of the past, he would suddenly interrupt his story with a blunt "that's none of your business." Lodin naturally became very curious.

Then in October 1951, the trial opened of Warrant Officer Andersson, the Soviet spy. Lodin noticed that Enbom was buying all the newspapers he could lay his hands on, reading reports of the case with minute attention, and becoming still more nervous. From time to time, he asked strange questions: "Do you know how an illegal group is organized?" "Do you know how a Soviet cipher system works?" And he seemed to be unreasonably frightened of meeting the police.

By now Lodin was quite clear that Enbom had been involved in some kind of clandestine activity—probably, he thought, during the war. But he was still confused and puzzled. He also noted that Enbom's attitude toward the communists was becoming more and more critical, that he had not rejoined a branch of the party in Stockholm since he came south again, and that he was no longer paying a subscription. So far as Lodin knew, Enbom's only contact with his former comrades at this time was one meeting with a communist Councillor, Artur Karlsson.

★   ★   ★

By now it was Christmas time. The Lodins and their guest celebrated Christmas Eve in the traditional Swedish way. The little flat was decorated gaily with greenery and tinsel, and at six o'clock they sat down to a big meal and glasses of Swedish schnapps. After dinner, came coffee and punch. At about nine, Lodin read aloud a short story by the "advanced" English poet and novelist Alex Comfort—an emotional (and, one might think, somewhat inappropriate) tale about the christening party of a child who had no legs. After the reading the three of them were sitting silent and in a sentimental mood, but—as Lodin afterwards insisted—"absolutely not drunk."

Suddenly Enbom started to tremble violently for no apparent reason. Then, in a strange, harsh voice his friends had never heard before, he began to pour out an extraordinary, hysterical story. Calling himself "Michael," he told them in a jumble of wild words that he was the head of a spy-ring, that Lodin's wife was a spy too—a member of his organization—that he would one day have on his conscience the deaths of twenty thousand innocent Swedes, and that he himself was now in mortal danger. He became terrified, then angry, then terrified again, and then he burst into tears. His two friends were astonished and very shocked.

In an effort to calm him, Lodin took him out for a short walk in the cold night air, and brought him in again for a drink of hot tea. But Enbom went on with his rambling, fantastic stories. Lodin took him for a second walk, but Enbom was still not calmed. Finally, at four in the morning, exhausted and amazed, Lodin retired to bed. Not surprisingly, he failed to sleep. He was convinced by now that Enbom had really been some kind of secret agent. But it was impossible even to begin to disentangle probable facts from the wild confusion of Enbom's hysterical outburst. It was plain that for a long time he had been living under great emotional pressure. But Lodin did not doubt that there was a large element of truth somewhere in his story.

Very late next morning, they breakfasted together. Enbom had evidently had some sleep and seemed to be calmer. But Lodin was worried because, while he was still in bed, Enbom had already visited neighbors who were well-known Communist Party members. What, he wondered, might not Enbom have said to them? And what would their reaction be?

Lodin decided that somehow he must get to the bottom of Enbom's story. "Last night you told us some very serious things," he remarked. "Do you remember?" Enbom at once looked up, pale and worried. Then he began talking again. "What would you think of a man who might be responsible for the deaths of twenty thousand women and children in northern Sweden?" he asked. And he added grimly, "People think the Kalix line (Sweden's northern defense line) is very strong. It is. But I can tell you that the Russians know just as much about it as the Swedish army does." Then he went on to give names and details of important strategic points in the north.

A little later, he and Lodin went out for another walk together and Enbom continued to make allusions to the activities which were weighing so heavily on his conscience. "Can you guess who is the man who is the chief of several spy-rings? Could you imagine that perhaps he is the very same man who looks at you from the little window at the entrance to the office of the Ny Dag?" A little later he gave the man's name: Artur

Karlsson, the Councillor, who was, in fact, working as watchman at the communist newspaper's office at that time. Then he made a vague reference to Lilian Ceder.

But that evening, over glasses of red wine, Enbom again became nervous and suspicious. He started telling another story, equally confused but rather different from the first. This time Lilian Ceder was the chief of a spy-ring. But Enbom repeated his earlier allegation that Lodin's wife, too, was a spy—a suggestion which Lodin knew was nonsense. He added that the Swedish police was full of communist agents. Lodin realized that Enbom was now scared by the possible consequences of his outbursts and was trying to ensure Lodin's silence.

For the whole of the next day—Boxing Day—Lodin worried and puzzled over the strange problem into which Enbom had plunged him. He became angry and confused himself and felt that he must talk to someone he could trust. He telephoned to a student friend, Roland Morrell, the President of the Swedish Social Democratic Youth, met him on December 27th at a small café near the central railway station, told him the whole story of Enbom's confession and asked for his advice. Morrell's first reaction was a natural one: that Lodin should go to the police. But, remembering Enbom's claim that there were communist agents in the police force, he decided that he would rather, as a first step, meet a political authority. Together, he and Morrell went to see the Minister of Defense. They had two preliminary interviews with the Minister and then a third, which Morrell did not attend but at which a high police officer was present.

For Lodin the situation was most troubling. He had until lately been a communist himself. His wife was still connected with the party—though she, too, left soon after. He was, moreover, betraying a friend. But the secret had evidently become so intolerable a burden to Enbom that he could not longer bear to keep it in. He was still afraid for himself—and perhaps for others—of the consequences of making a full confession. But for a man in his state of mind, a full confession was clearly the only possible solution. Besides, the matter was apparently of grave importance. Lodin decided that it was his duty to give what help he could to the police.

But for the police, too, it was a complicated problem. From their questioning of Lodin and the early investigations which followed, it seemed that they were indeed on the track of something exceedingly important. But, as yet, they had no sort of proof. If they arrested Enbom at once (and at first it was even doubtful whether they had sufficient grounds to do so), he might easily refuse to talk. And others, connected with him, might be warned. They decided to work cautiously and slowly.

It was Lodin's task to try first to persuade Enbom that it was in his own interest to confess. This he failed to do. Enbom was too frightened to take so critical a decision. Then Lodin must try to make Enbom give him more details. He succeeded to some extent in this: Enbom marked a map with the positions of defenses in the north of Sweden, and wrote down some notes about a code he said he had been given. Meanwhile, Lodin saw Lilian Ceder. At first she became afraid and burst into tears. But eventually she agreed to meet and talk to the police. But she also talked to a communist friend: and the information she gave that friend was passed on to the Communist Party. A little later, Enbom himself called at the office of the *Ny Dag*. He was applying for a job as a proof-reader with another Stockholm daily paper and (with extraordinary optimism, it seems) hoped for a reference from his old comrades. It was not surprising that he got no answer.

On February 12th, 1952, Enbom, who was still living at the Lodin's flat, was arrested in the street nearby. This can hardly have come as much of a surprise. Probably he was already half expecting it. In his heart, he must have known that it was the only possible ending to his troubles. At all events, when, a little later, he made his full confession, he found at long last the relief which his bursting conscience had been seeking. And he bore no grudge towards Jan Lodin. "You acted in the only possible way," he told him afterwards, "and I am grateful for what you did." Lilian Ceder was arrested on the same day.

★   ★   ★

Enbom's story, when he told it to the police, was less wild and melodramatic than he had made it sound at his first breakdown on Christmas Eve. But it was quite as grave as Lodin suspected. It started more than ten years before, in the summer of 1941.

At that time Sweden—who had reaffirmed her traditional neutrality when the war began—was isolated from the western world. In the spring of 1940, the Germans had occupied Denmark and Norway. Sweden was at the mercy of the German blockade and no one knew when she, too, might not fall a victim to Hitler's armies. Soon afterward the Germans had put pressure on the Swedish Government to allow the passage of war material and limited numbers of soldiers on leave to and from Norway by rail through Sweden. On July 8th, 1940, Sweden had reluctantly agreed—on condition that the material and men travelled in sealed trains and that the number of German soldiers passing through into Norway should not be more than those coming out. After the German attack on Russia in June 1941, the German Government demanded more concessions, the most important being that Sweden should allow the passage of one fully armed German division from Norway to Finland. Again, Sweden agreed, with the explicit declaration that this concession would not be repeated—though the split in the Swedish Government caused by this decision almost broke up the national coalition then in power. The German transit traffic of troops on leave continued until August 1943.

Meanwhile, the Swedish communists had been performing the same acrobatics as their comrades in other countries. At the beginning of 1939 they were campaigning against Swedish neutrality. On August 20th they denounced rumors of a Nazi-Soviet Pact as "Goebbels-inspired propaganda." Six days later, they hailed that Pact as a "great victory for peace." They then began to support neutrality. Soon after the war started, their leader, Hilding Hagberg, declared: "The present war is not an ideological war, not a war of democracy against fascism, but an imperialistic war for world supremacy and markets." Even the invasion of the two neighboring countries failed to shake them. "Through Germany's occupation of Denmark and Norway we are excluded from the world's seas and isolated in the German sphere. . . . But we cannot wish that we were in any other situation," they declared. Even eleven days before the German attack on Russia, they were still campaigning against the Western allies. On June 11th, 1941, *Ny Dag* wrote: "The war now being fought is an imperialist war for world supremacy and for the means to exploit other peoples. Big business is behind the blood of the battlefield and the tears of the home. The biggest gains will be made by the dollar magnates on the staff of Roosevelt." But when Russia was invaded and suddenly became an ally of the West, they immediately changed their line. The Soviet Union, Britain and America, they announced, were fighting "a just war of liberation against barbaric fascist hordes." The German military transit traffic across the north of Sweden then became a subject for loud protests by the Swedish Communist Party, and of great practical interest to the Russians. It was at this stage that Enbom embarked on his career as a spy.

He was working at this time on the railway at Boden, along which the German military trains were passing. One day, his landlord, a communist sympathizer, gave him a message: Per Ekman, a Communist Party member and the Boden correspondent of the *Norrskensflamman* had asked to see him. At the office, Enbom was introduced to an older man whom he had never met before, named Sven Jonsson. Jonsson was working as a travelling bookseller for the Communist Party publishing house, *Arbetarkultur*. He asked Enbom if he would watch the German transit trains and make reports. This seemed a relatively simple task, for every truck was labelled with its place of origin and destination, those carrying troops each had a capacity of forty men, and it was sometimes possible to identify the freight carried on the others. Enbom agreed, and Jonsson said he would collect the reports in due course.

A few weeks later, another salesman from *Arbetarkultur* arrived in Boden: Artur Karlsson, the communist Councillor and veteran Communist Party member. Karlsson began by showing him his books, but Enbom declined to buy. Then Karlsson mentioned that he had heard that Sven Jonsson had asked Enbom for "some information." Enbom gave his first report and Karlsson took notes. But Karlsson seemed dissatisfied and told him to be more accurate in future. Exact figures were required for the number of trucks carrying men, material, guns, dismantled aircraft and so on, and an estimate of what type of traffic was increasing and what decreasing. Karlsson showed him how to keep notes in code, disguised as grocery bills. He also told Enbom to expand the sources of his information and, as a start, to go to the station at Gällivare, 100 miles away on another line, where a railwayman named Petterson would be ready to help him. If Karlsson could not come himself to collect the next report, Enbom would be approached by a new contact-man. The passwords would be as follows. The contact-man: "Do you wish to buy a fountain pen?" Enbom: "No, but I need a new nib." Contact-man: "What make?" Enbom: "Pelican number three." After this talk with Karlsson, Enbom clearly understood that the work he was being asked to do was illegal and that the information was to be passed to Russia. But probably in his own mind he still thought of it rather as service to the wider communist cause than as espionage for a foreign country. As a loyal Communist Party member his chief loyalty was naturally to "the first country of socialism." And after all, a war was being fought. At all events, at this stage his conscience was quite clear.

It was many months, however, before Enbom was able to visit Gällivare. He did not get leave from his work at Boden until June 1942. He found Petterson, who had evidently been told to expect him and was prepared to help him, but whose information was very vague. Enbom warned him that he would want a fuller, more exact report next time. Later that summer, Enbom was transferred from Boden to Bjurå, on the railway 25 miles to the north-east. Here, in October, Karlsson called on him again.

He brought important news. So far, although Enbom's

reports were doubtless of some interest to the Russians, the tasks he had been set seem also to have been treated partly as preliminary tests. Evidently he had passed those tests to their satisfaction. For Karlsson now explained that Enbom was to have direct contact with a man in Stockholm—a Russian, he hinted. He would also be given a wireless transmitter in order to signal reports straight from northern Sweden to the Soviet Union. Karlsson asked Enbom to arrange to come to Stockholm during the following February. Meanwhile he told him to continue to collect information about the German transit traffic. Then, he gave him 100 crowns to cover the expenses (he explained) of Enbom's coming journey to Stockholm. This was the first money Enbom took for spying.

On February 21st, 1943, Enbom was given two weeks' leave of absence from his work. Using his railwayman's pass, he travelled down to Stockholm and went straight to Artur Karlsson's flat. Karlsson left him there while he went out to find his Russian contact-man. When he returned he told Enbom to meet him later at Djurgårdsbron, a bridge which takes the road and trolley lines over from the main part of the city to the island of Djurgården, on which stand the fairground and open-air museum of Skansen, beside a thickly wooded park.

Enbom met Karlsson on the bridge at the appointed time. Together they sauntered slowly along a path beside the water towards a little, secluded promontory on the north shore of the island, the haunt of courting couples from whom it takes its name—Kärleksudden, "The Point of Love." As they approached, Karlsson pointed out to Enbom a solitary, waiting figure; then he turned and walked away. Enbom went forward alone to meet the Russian. His career as a direct Soviet agent had begun.

Hairpin on the Fence

★

Enbom was never able to identify the stranger whom he met in the park at Djurgården. He was a short, dark, sturdily built man, about forty-five years old, and Enbom was certain that he was a Russian diplomat. But he did not introduce himself and Enbom never knew a name for him. He spoke good Swedish with no noticeable accent.

The Russian's first questions were a matter of routine. He followed the usual Soviet procedure for recruiting foreign spies. He questioned Enbom closely about his life and career, and asked him to prepare a complete autobiographical dossier and a portrait photograph: these were to be sent in due course to Moscow for checking and approval. Then he warned Enbom of the need for secrecy: he must say nothing to his family or fiancée (he was now engaged to be married the following May), he must have no further contact with Artur Karlsson or with any other communists whom he knew to be working for the Russians, and he must find a convincing pretext for his journeys to Stockholm and, if possible, avoid meeting people who knew him while he was there. He must not worry about the risks he would be taking because if anything happened to him, the Russian said, his family would be looked after.

Meanwhile, he was to continue watching the German transit traffic as before. The Russian heard his report of information he had collected since Artur Karlsson's visit to him at Bjurå, and then warned him that for the time being he would report orally and must keep only the briefest notes. In due course, he would be given a wireless transmitter for communicating directly with Russia, and meanwhile would be taught a secret cipher. Next, the Russian settled arrangements for their future meetings. He would normally be available, he said, in the late afternoon on the second Sunday of each month. For all meetings he would wait for Enbom at a shed belonging to the Albano rowing club on the shore of the Brunnsviken lake in a park to the northwest of the city. In case a colleague should take the Russian's place, Enbom must have a copy of the picture magazine *Se* showing from his pocket, and they would use the "Pelican number three" passwords he had already been taught by Artur Karlsson. Then the Russian handed him 400 crowns for which Enbom wrote out a receipt and signed it "Michael," which the Russian told him was to be his cover-name. Finally, the Russian took him across Stockholm and showed him the Albano boat club meeting-place.

★ ★ ★

Enbom stayed on in Stockholm for two more days and then went back to work at Bjurå. There he continued to watch the German transit trains while he wrote out the life story which the Russian wanted. But he was unable to get leave for the meeting in Stockholm on the second Sunday in April, and when he eventually arrived at the end of the month, he failed, for some reason, to find the Russian. Despite his instructions, he then telephoned to Artur Karlsson. They met at Karlsson's flat, and took a bus together to the north of the city, where Enbom got out and, following Karlsson's instructions, found the Russian waiting for him. Together they walked over to the boat club while Enbom made his report and handed over the photograph and dossier about himself. The Russian again paid Enbom and took a receipt signed "Michael."

Enbom was married on May 9th. He told his wife nothing of his spy work either then or later. His next visit to Stockholm was in mid-August. He brought his wife with him and stayed for six days. During that time he had three meetings with the Russian. At the first of these, Enbom made his last report on the German transit traffic which ended a few days later. But he also added, for the first time, a report about purely Swedish military matters. From his brother Martin, who was then doing his second period of service in the army in the Tornedalen in northern Sweden, he had collected information about troops and defenses in that area. Enbom had not been asked for this information: he volunteered it on his own initiative to impress his masters with his keenness and usefulness. Besides, he realized that, with the stopping of the German trains, his first assignment was now finished. The Russian showed great interest, told him that further reports of this kind were needed, and asked him a number of specific questions (the details of which, for security reasons, were afterwards kept secret by the Swedish Government). At this moment Enbom must have lost his last illusions—if indeed he ever had any—about the nature of his work. Until now, despite the fact that he was being paid, he could perhaps have made himself believe that his spying on the Germans was a patriotic service, aimed at the defeat of fascism which indirectly threatened his own country. But now no make-believe could hide the fact that selling secrets of his own country's defenses to the Russian Embassy was plain, straightforward treason.

At his second meeting during the August visit Enbom was taught a cipher. The system was the same as that used by Richard Sorge and other Soviet spies. The cipher was based on a tourist book called *A Week In Skåne* and the key word was *Stavanger*. Enbom learned to use the cipher in a few hours. The next day, August 18th, he met the Russian again for the third time and was given a wireless transmitter camouflaged in a brown suitcase (like one of the sets used by Nicholas Vavoudes). Inside it were instructions in Norwegian, and also a Belgian-made pistol. The Russian told Enbom that he must try himself to find an operator—a "pianist"—for the set. Enbom said that this would certainly not be easy but that he would do his best. He took the suitcase to the central station and left it in the luggage-room. He spent the next three days in Stockholm with his wife and then returned with her to Bjurå. Shortly before leaving, in order to avoid arousing her suspicions, he registered the suitcase through to Boden station where he afterwards collected it, checked its contents and hid it temporarily in a pit in the forest nearby. Later he took it unobtrusively to his home and hid it there. But—not surprisingly perhaps—he failed to find an operator.

Enbom did not return to Stockholm until mid-October, and he had little to report. But when he met the Russian at the boat club he found him with a second man. This, the Russian explained, was his successor, he himself was soon going home. He said good-bye to Enbom and thanked him for his work. As before, no names were mentioned, but Enbom later identified the new man as

Fedor Grigorievich Chernov, a secretary at the Soviet Legation who had arrived in Stockholm some three years before. Of all the Russians Enbom worked for, he was to get to like Chernov best. He was kind to him and friendly, Enbom said, and also extremely clever. Like his predecessor, he spoke good Swedish.

Chernov at once set about reorganizing the arrangements for Enbom's work. First he met him near Dragonsgården, in a wide, rolling open space to the east of the city, with clumps of birch and fir trees. This was to be their new rendezvous. Then he walked with him out to an isolated place at the far end of the Djurgårdsbrunn canal where, in a lonely, wooded spot near the seashore, was a heap of rocks. Chernov pointed out a small cavity and told Enbom that he would place there a tin pencil box. From this box, reports, instructions or money could be collected without their meeting.

Next Chernov arranged a simple signal system. On the northern edge of the city, about half a mile from the Soviet Embassy building, is the Östermalm sports ground. Round it runs a high wire fence. On the pavement outside this fence, at the southern corner of the sports ground, stands a green telephone box. Chernov explained to Enbom that whenever he had put a report in the pencil box, he must wind a thin hairpin into a spiral and hook it on to the fence at a point just to the right of the telephone box. He also told him that early on the morning of any day when Chernov was expecting to meet him, he should confirm that he was in Stockholm and would keep the appointment by hanging a hairpin in the same place but this time bent into a loop. In this way, Chernov would avoid having to make unnecessary journeys to the meeting-place or to the "letter box."

Unless otherwise arranged, the regular meetings would take place, as before, on the second Sunday of each month. But Chernov later arranged that, if he wanted to summon Enbom to Stockholm for a special meeting, or to cancel one already arranged, he could send a postcard to his home. The text of the card would be unimportant, the message would be in the signature and postmark. A woman's name would mean that Enbom must come to Stockholm for the next regular meeting, a man's name that the next meeting had been cancelled. If the card was postmarked from Uppsala is would be particularly urgent for Enbom to come south. Altogther Enbom received three of these cards. They all read *Cannot come. Greetings. Elsa.*

With these practical details settled, Chernov now turned to Enbom's next assignment. He was to report in detail on the condition and morale of troops in northern Sweden, to provide full sets of press cuttings from the local papers on military matters, to report orally on military manœuvers, to supply general information about new fortifications, to organize a network of military spies, and, finally, make new efforts to find a wireless operator. Chernov then gave Enbom his usual bribe and sent him back to Bjurå.

*   *   *

In the next three years, Enbom made eleven more journeys to Stockholm to report to Chernov: one that December, four in 1944, and three each in 1945 and 1946. To his wife and friends, he explained these and later journeys by saying that he was now writing a book and had to have discussions with a publisher. On each occasion he gave whatever military information he had been able to collect, and each time he was paid 400 or 500 crowns.

In September 1946, Enbom travelled down to Stockholm for his twelfth meeting with Chernov. It was to be the last, for Chernov was due to leave for Russia some months later and now handed Enbom over to his third Russian master, Peter Zavaroukhin, a captain in the Soviet Military Attaché's office. Zavaroukhin made no changes in Enbom's methods of work, but, for more than a year, their meetings lapsed. In November 1947, a postcard from *Elsa* summoned Enbom to Stockholm, but when he duly arrived on the second Sunday of December. Zavaroukhin failed to appear at the meeting-place. This was a minor disaster for Enbom who was extremely short of money at the time. Early the next year, 1948, Enbom received a letter from Artur Karlsson which indicated that the Russians again wanted to see him. He met Zavaroukhin on the following second Sunday, and again in mid-July. At each of these meetings he made his usual reports and was paid his usual bribe, and at the second meeting he was handed over to yet another Russian.

This was Captain (later Major) Victor Mihailovich Egorov, the new Soviet Deputy Military Attaché who had arrived in Stockholm only a month before. Enbom disliked Egorov: "a hard man" he afterwards said, who had a rough, military manner and always spoke to him in orders. Part of the difficulty, perhaps, was that Egorov spoke no Swedish so that their conversations were carried on in German. But the very fact that Enbom was put in direct contact with this relatively senior Soviet official showed that, despite the irregularity of Enbom's meetings with Zavaroukhin, the Russians were still extremely interested in his work.

His first task from Egorov, however, was undramatic. Having checked that Enbom remembered the hairpin signal, the "letter box," the postcard code and the meet-

ing times, he told him that he intended to change the
rendezvous to a new place on the far side of Stockholm: a telephone box in a street in the suburb of Mid-
sommarkransen. To satisfy himself that Enbom could
find the place, he sent him out there that evening with
instructions to wait until Egorov walked past and, as
a signal that he had recognized Enbom, blow his nose.
Enbom duly went to the telephone box, watched the
Russian blow his nose, and left for home. Over the
next two and a half years, Enbom made eight further
journeys to Stockholm on Egorov's instructions and met
him six times, bringing his total number of meetings
with Soviet officials to twenty-six.

A part of the information which Enbom stole for the
Russians on these occasions, and most of the details,
have been kept unpublished by the Swedish Government for reasons of security. But the published documents alone make it clear that his reports covered a
great deal of ground. They always included observations on the general state of military preparedness in
northern Sweden on the strength and morale of local
units, and on recent manœuvers. Likewise, Enbom always handed over a collection of cuttings from the
local press dealing with defense. But the bulk of his
reports was devoted to giving the location and description of defense lines, fortifications and military installations of all kinds, ranging from airfields and strategic
roads to gun sites and tank traps. He took a special
interest in the movement and storing of supplies, equipment and ammunition, and he very often included maps
and sketches. He added a certain amount of information
—which it was relatively easy for him, as a linesman,
to get, and in which the Russians showed great interest
—on the layout of railway tracks and stations, of which
he stole a number of blueprints from his employers.

During most of the time that he was spying, Enbom
was convinced that a war between Russia and the non-
communist Powers was imminent and that Sweden
would be invaded by Russian troops who would attack
across the Finnish frontier. The Russians whom he met
did nothing to discourage this view. On the contrary,
they encouraged him to concentrate on collecting military information which could only be of interest to a
potential invader. And more than once they asked for
special reports on airfields and unobstructed areas for
landing troops.

To provide so great a variety of information, Enbom
gradually built up a small network of informants. The
first of these was his own brother, from whom he first
passed some information to his original Russian master
in 1943. Martin was two years younger than Fritiof
Enbom, and had had less schooling than his brother,
whom he admired as a better educated, more intellectual man. He was influenced by Fritiof's political views
and had been one of the founders of the Boden Young
Communist League. But though Fritiof had urged him
to do so, he never actually became a card-carrying
member of the Communist Party itself, although he
did once stand for a local election on the Communist
Party list. He had had a series of varied—and mostly
badly paid—jobs and had been refused permanent employment on the railway on physical grounds. But he
was called up for three periods of military service in the
infantry regiment based on Boden: from May 1941 until November 1942, during the summer of 1943 and
again during 1944. For part of this time he was in the
regiment's headquarters company at Boden. He had a
good army record, and he eventually became a sergeant.
But early in 1944 he was convicted by a civil court for
offences against rationing regulations and for receiving

ration cards, and was fined 75 crowns. He asked his brother to lend him the money, but was told that he had none to spare. A few days later, however, Fritiof went down on one of his visits to Stockholm and on his return handed Martin the 75 crowns. Later, when Martin asked about repayment, Fritiof told him he did not want the money back but that Martin "could help him in other ways." From then on, Martin supplied him with considerable amounts of military information which he picked up during his army service. Fritiof also asked him for a personal dossier about himself which he said "they" wanted in Stockholm. Martin quite clearly understood how the information he was giving was to be used.

★   ★   ★

At about the same time, Fritiof Enbom made another journey over to Gällivare to reestablish contact with Petterson, the railwayman with whom Karlsson had originally put him in touch. Petterson's information seems to have been of limited use, but Enbom told Chernov about him and Chernov asked him for the usual biographical dossier and photograph. But to avoid making a special journey to Gällivare, Enbom gave Chernov, at their next meeting, a photograph of some quite different person—this was, incidentally, the only occasion (and hardly a very serious one) on which Enbom is known deliberately to have misled his Russian masters.

The next recruit to his group of spies was a neighbor and fellow railway worker named Fingal Larsson, whom Enbom much impressed as a "learned man." They became friendly in 1942, and two years later they set up a local Communist Party branch at Bjurå of which Enbom was chairman and Larsson treasurer. But it was a small affair for there were only thirteen houses at Bjurå and the branch membership never exceeded half a dozen. In the spring of 1946, Enbom took Larsson into his confidence. He showed him his transmitter and told him about his journeys to Stockholm. Larsson began to provide information on defense works, fortifications and military communications.

In May of the following year, 1947, Enbom left the railway, and took a job as Boden correspondent of the *Norrskensflamman.* In May 1949 he was transferred to the head office of that paper at Luleå. In many ways, his new employment made it easier for him to spy: he could travel more freely and his journeys to Stockholm were probably less likely to arouse comment. But he was bady paid and continued to be very short of money. How far his colleagues at the *Norrskensflamman* knew of or suspected his spying is not clear, but one of the members of his group was associated with that paper and later joined its staff. This was Hugo Gjerswold, a twenty-seven-year-old communist who was Chairman of the Boden branch of the Young Communist League in 1946 and later became a full member of the party. He was useful to Enbom because he had served as a gunner, and later as a noncommissioned officer, in the artillery regiment based on Boden for over five years— having joined as a volunteer when he was sixteen—and was then employed as a civilian by various local military units. In his spare time, he worked as a subscription collector for the *Norrskensflamman,* which was why he had called at the paper's Boden office and met Enbom.

Gjerswold made it clear that he was dissatisfied with his job as a driver at the local artillery headquarters, and Enbom gradually let him into the secret of his work, showed him his wireless transmitter and took from him a personal dossier of particulars for the Russians. He was well placed to pick up or overhear all kinds of useful information, and had some access to military maps. Enbom considered him intelligent but found him nervous. He refused Enbom's suggestion that he should learn to work the transmitter (Enbom had still not found an operator) on account of the danger involved. But he was apparently encouraged when Enbom assured him that, even if they were caught while spying and exposed to the contempt of their countrymen, they would "be liberated when the Russians won the coming war and given jobs at 50,000 crowns a year."

The next person to be associated with Enbom's spy-ring was in a rather different position from the others. Though Lilian Ceder was an active communist and admired Enbom for spying, her motive for joining him—like his asking her to do so—was personal, and the information she gave him was of no real importance. From the sheltered childhood of a schoolteacher's home in southern Sweden, she had escaped in 1938, at the age of seventeen, to Stockholm, where she first became a nursemaid and then took a series of badly paid jobs as a typist. She became tubercular and spent part of several years at sanatoria or hospitals. In 1940 she got to know some young communists, began to go to their meetings and read their literature and, in January 1943, joined the Young Communist League. But her new comrades never really accepted her. They despised her for her middle-class background—"a remnant from the ninetenth century who studies French, plays the piano and does embroidery: furthermore, she wears a fur coat," one of them commented later. Nevertheless she did her best to impress them as a good proletarian, and in 1945 she took a job as an office girl at the *Ny Dag*. Here she met a communist journalist named Ture Eriksson who told her that he had once been jailed for illegal activities. She was greatly impressed, romanticized him as a hero, and fell in love. But Eriksson was married, his wife reacted, and to escape from an unsatisfactory situation she applied, at the end of 1947, for a job as a "volunteer" (a learner working for almost no pay) on the staff of the *Norrskensflamman,* and went north to Luleå in January 1948. At first she was lonely: "Families don't generally invite girls who are alone," she later complained, "it is only the bachelors that they take care of." But soon she was once again in very much the same situation which she had sought to escape from in Stockholm.

Enbom first got to know her by telephone when he rang through to his paper's office from Boden. Then, that autumn, he met her at a Communist Party meeting at Luleå. He made a great impression on her. "He had exactly the same interests as me, exactly the same opinion on women's questions. His great interest was journalism and he was also interested in poetry, writing short stories and matters of art," she said later. And she added, "In Enbom I found a friend to whom I could always go when I was in trouble, a person who could always answer my questions, a person who would always encourage and never blame. He was tolerant and almost as understanding as a woman . . . this was the kind of friendship I had been longing for all my life." She became his mistress and he began to tell her of his illegal work—although whether he did so to use her, or to insure her silence by compromising her, is not clear. At all events, he said that he was the leader of a spy-ring, showed her his transmitter (which she eventually agreed to learn to operate; though she never did so) and later informed her that he had told the Russians about her and that she was now a member of his group. Thereafter she did, from time to time, give him small items of information which she thought might be of use.

The last person whom Enbom is known to have tried to recruit to his spy-ring was the only one not directly connected with the Communist Party—and, as it turned out, he was a failure. His name was Tage Wickström. In September 1950, Enbom made the following observations about him in his notebook: "Tage Wickström, supervisor at the building department of the Fortifications Administration. Lives at Kyrkgatan, Boden, works at office in grounds of Garrison Hospital. Born 1918, married, two children. Expert on the Kalix line which he helped to construct. Is now concerned with calculating costs for all military building. Has already given information unwittingly. Is a sympathizer, but the main thing is that he has a sense of economy. Will certainly give information as long as he is paid for it. Absolutely reliable."

Enbom had first met Wickström as a contributor to the sports pages of the *Norrskenflamman* in 1947. He had visited his home and had learned that Wickström was in correspondence with someone living behind the Iron Curtain whom he apparently hoped to help to escape to Sweden. This made Enbom wonder if Wickström might not respond to another kind of bribery besides money. They met again by chance in Stockholm in March 1950 when Enbom was there to see Egorov, and Wickström was on a short visit. Enbom explained that he was in contact with the Russians who had once offered him a journey to the Soviet Union. If Wickström could do them some favor, the Russians might allow him to visit his friends in the East or even let them come to Sweden. Enbom added that there was an easier way of earning extra money than by writing on sport for local papers. At first Wickström seemed interested, and

Enbom told Egorov of him. The Russian asked for the usual personal dossier and photograph. But Enbom quickly found that Wickström was only prepared to sell information which was false. He met him on only two subsequent occasions and never gave him any money.

Enbom's belief that war was imminent and that there would soon be a Soviet invasion of northern Sweden, led him in 1948 to consider plans for giving the Russians more practical assistance than spying when the moment came. He assumed that the capture of the Boden fortress would be a major Russian objective and felt, he later said, that it would be "criminal negligence" not to help them by obstructing Swedish mobilization, troop movements and communications, destroying certain military installations and smuggling fifth columnists into key points. It might be possible, he thought, to organize a group of some two hundred potential quislings among communist railwaymen and civilians working for the army. He discussed these plans in detail with Hugo Gjerswold. How far he also discussed them with Egorov is not clear; nor is it publicly known what stage his preparations reached. But he did later formally confess to "preparing for high treason."

★   ★   ★

Once his meetings with his Russian masters in Stockholm had become a regular routine, Enbom normally took his instructions only from them. But his original contact-man, Artur Karlsson, did appear briefly in the story twice more: once at Bjurå in 1945, when he told Enbom that he was arranging "with another person" to find him a wireless operator (though one was never found), and once at the *Norrskensflamman* office at Luleå in 1948, when he told him of some military infor-

mation he had happened to pick up. This Enbom—
remembering his orders not to have dealings with other
Swedes connected with Soviet espionage—did not pass
on. Then, in the late summer of 1950, a prominent local
communist visited the *Norrskensflamman* office with a
Russian Enbom had not met before. This was Victor
Anissimov, the Stockholm *Tass* correspondent and the
first master of Hilding Andersson, the Swedish naval
spy. Later that day Anissimov told Enbom that he
wanted a private talk with him and took him for a walk.
He explained that he had greetings for "Michael" and
added, "We want to see you in Stockholm at Telefon-
plan"—a square not far from his normal rendezvous
with Egorov. He named a day and time, gave Enbom
100 crowns to cover his fare and took the usual signed
receipt. It seems that the change of meeting-place was
the reason why the message was sent by Anissimov instead of in the usual postcard from *Elsa*. Anissimov's
brief talk with Enbom was, incidentally, the only known
direct, personal link between the two big Swedish spy
cases.

Enbom's last meeting with Egorov—his twenty-sixth
with a Soviet official—was on April 8th, 1951. On the
evening of the 7th he flew down from Luleå to Stockholm and in the morning fixed the usual looped hairpin to
the wire fence at Östermalm sports ground. That afternoon he handed over negatives of photographs of
a sketch he had made of an airfield and gave a usual
report about the military situation in the north with
details about recent fortification works. He then returned to Luleå. Enbom himself claims that after that
meeting, he did no more spying and had no further
contact with any Russian. Some months later, he received a postcard from *Elsa* which he ignored. He did
not revisit the meeting-places nor the "letter box" at

Djurgårdsbrunn. In May, he left the *Norrskensflamman* and went south to Stockholm where he found work at a factory making dairy equipment. That autumn he went to live with the Lodins.

★   ★   ★

Precisely what made Enbom cease spying when he did is still something of a puzzle. His motives were certainly mixed, as indeed they were throughout this story—except perhaps at the very beginning when he may well have felt no qualms about spying on the German trains. He himself said that he began to get disillusioned with the Communist Party and the methods of the Russians at the time of the communist coup in Czechoslovakia in February 1948. But by that time he had already been spying for nearly seven years and to make a break was not so easy. Besides he was then—as he habitually was—very short of money: though it seems doubtful whether the bribes the Russians gave him—the equivalent of some 175 dollars a year—ever covered much more than his travelling expenses. Probably personal reasons played a part in his final decision. Even Egorov's brusque, cold manner may have been a small contributory cause. Meanwhile, his wife was divorcing him, Lilian Ceder was no longer his mistress and he was in trouble with the parents of a local girl. He was anxious to get away from Luleå. But no doubt he decided only after months of hesitation—just as he hesitated before making his first outburst to the Lodins and hesitated again, after his arrest in February 1952, before he made a full confession.

He admitted to the police at once his connection with his various Russian masters, the last of whom, Egorov (warned, perhaps, by the Communist Party), had left for Russia three weeks before Enbom's arrest. After a week or two, he also told them about Artur Karlsson. But for two months he refused to say anything about the members of his group—the people he had himself recruited and for whom, perhaps, he felt personally responsible.

Gradually, however, the evidence was pieced together, and Enbom eventually made a clean breast of the whole story. Six days after his arrest, he was taken out to Djurgårdsbrunn and showed the police the "letter box." In a tin pencil case they found 1,000 crowns in 100- and 50-crown notes: a "bonus" awarded after his last report or, perhaps, an extra bribe to persuade him to continue spying. Then the wireless set, the pistol and a suitcase full of his notes were found at Luleå.

Lilian Ceder was arrested on the same day as Enbom. The arrests followed of Gjerswold on March 10th, Artur Karlsson on March 31st, Fingal Larsson and Enbom's brother Martin on April 7th, and of Tage Wickström on May 13. The trial opened in the Stockholm Magistrate's Court on June 16th and sentence was given on July 31st. All the prisoners except Wickström were found guilty; three appealed: Karlsson, Larsson and Gjerswold. The appeals of Karlsson and Larsson eventually reached the Supreme Court and the case was not closed until that Court gave judgment on March 24th 1953. The final sentences were as follows: Fritiof Enbom, imprisonment for life with hard labor (the heaviest Swedish penalty) for espionage, gross espionage, preparations for high treason and preparations for espionage; Hugo Gjerswold, hard labor for life for espionage and gross espionage; Martin Enbom, seven years' hard labor for espionage; Artur Karlsson, three years' hard labor for complicity in espionage; Fingal Larsson, two years' hard labor for espionage; Lilian Ceder, eight months' hard labor for assisting in espionage.

★   ★   ★

Swedish public opinion, already alarmed by the Andersson case less than a year before, was deeply shocked
by the revelations made at Enbom's trial. The Government protested sharply to the Soviet Ambassador in
Stockholm about the activities of members of his staff.
The reputation of the Swedish communists was dam-
aged even more severely than by the Andersson case,
because Enbom himself and all his convicted associates
had been so closely associated with their party at the
time that they were spying. Nevertheless they loudly
denounced the trial as a propaganda fake which they
variously attributed to the influence of President Truman (who, they said, ordered it), to the leader of the
parliamentary opposition Professor Ohlin, to the ruling
Social-Democratic Party, to "reactionary" police officials. They alleged that it was yet another case of
"provocation," and that Enbom had invented all the
evidence because he was insane.

The first of these two allegations hardly tallied with
the proud claim of one of Enbom's colleagues on the
Norrskensflamman named Helmer Persson who wrote,
in November 1949, while Enbom was still actually running his spy-ring from the *Norrskensflamman* office,
that in the "communist fortress" in northern Sweden
". . . we have been able to eliminate the class enemy
and to keep the party free from class enemies and provocateurs."

Nor did the charge of insanity carry great conviction,
although the Communist Party did inspire a group of
three sympathetic doctors—who, incidentally, had never
seen Enbom—to sign a "report" to that effect. The prison
psychiatrist, who later subjected him to exhaustive tests

and had him under observation for twelve days, declared that there was no trace of mental disease or of any state compatible with insanity, but that on the contrary, Enbom was an unusually intelligent man.

Meanwhile, the Soviet Government's reaction was identical with that of the Swedish Communist Party. In two statements to the Swedish Foreign Minister, it rejected his Government's protests on the grounds that they were "based on false statements made by provocateurs whose object it is to slander members of the Soviet Embassy staff and to impair good-neighbor relations between Sweden and the Soviet Union," and added that since the verdict of the Stockholm Magistrate's Court "as is well known, is founded on the perjury of Enbom and other police agents, a sentence passed on the grounds of such material cannot inspire confidence."

Of all Enbom's convicted fellow prisoners, the only one who remained defiant and protested his innocence throughout (and apparently still does) was Artur Karlsson, the man who was perhaps more responsible than any of the others but who paradoxically—because it was not proved that he himself had spied—received one of the lightest sentences.

Fritiof Enbom will remain in prison for at least ten years. After that he can ask to be released provided that his conduct in jail has been exemplary. He works in the printing shop and on the prison newspaper and is again busy with a book. Those who know him best say that he is now as happy as it is possible for a life-sentence prisoner to be. He is paying for his crime, and the burden of his guilt is no longer on his conscience.

Some Conclusions

★

This book is mainly a book of facts. The comment and interpretation, where it occurs, is incidental to the main story of the five spy cases. The summary which follows discusses some points which those cases raise.

The cases show, quite clearly, a uniformity of Russian methods: and it is, after all, only natural that such matters as recruiting, supervising and bribing spies, and arranging secret meetings, codes and passwords, should have become part of a routine technique. The case which follows the general pattern least closely is the Greek case: and that is to be expected because there Russian supervision was indirect.

Where there is no uniformity at all is in the reactions of the Russians when one of their spy-rings is broken up. In the Sorge case, they said nothing whatever. In Canada they admitted that their actions had been "inadmissible" but claimed that the information stolen was of no interest. In Greece, some of their spies were hailed as martyrs and others—just as devoted—were denounced as filthy traitors. And in Sweden they blandly asserted that both cases had been invented and that one of their leading spies was mad.

In each of the five cases, it was the Communist Party which prepared and "developed" the spies and supplied them to the Russians. Without the Communist Party none of those five cases could have happened.

In some of the cases there is a curious personal similarity about the spies themselves—just as there is usually
a curious personal similarity, in appearance and manner,
among other communists throughout the world. With
some exceptions, they are mediocre, limited and dull
people. "A little grey man" was how Andersson was
described to me by someone who had watched him
closely for some time. He said that that applied to Enbom too, though Enbom was also disorganized and
dissolute. The wife of a fellow scientist told me that
the description perfectly fitted Doctor Nunn May,
whose dullness was such that she had once burst into
tears after entertaining him at dinner. Even the Greeks,
when I watched them at their trial, seemed much less
interesting than the dramatic circumstances of their
case had led me to expect. Klausen and de Voukelitch
were dull men, too, though clearly Sorge was not.

In the popular imagination, scientists who spy tend
to become glamourized because of the mystery and
drama attributed to their work. In fact, they seem to
have no very special personal characteristics, and their
motives for spying seem to be no different from those
of the other communists. But they are in a slightly different category from the others to the extent that the
great secrecy of their work imposes special responsibilities upon them, responsibilities which sometimes
neither their character nor their training has fitted them
to carry. Some of the scientists in this book, like May,
argued afterward that all they had intended to do was
to "pool" scientific information among allies. The Canadian, Mazerall, said, "I did not like the idea of supplying information. It was put to me not so much that I
was supplying information to the Soviet Government,
either. It was more that, as scientists, we were pooling
information, and I actually asked him (his communist

contact-man) if we could hope to find this reciprocal."
But they all realized, of course, that there was no question at all of "reciprocity;" and they also realized that the only reason why the Russians wanted them to steal scientific information was to be able to make new weapons for possible use against their own countries in a future war. For, as communists, they firmly believed the Russian thesis that a clash between the communist and non-communist Powers must inevitably come.

★ ★ ★

All the spy-rings mentioned in this book were, of course, failures in the end—in the sense, that is, that they were eventually discovered and broken up. But some of them were highly successful for many years. And, for the handfuls of spies who have been caught, there must be very many others still at work. The scope of the cases we do know of, together with what we may reasonably guess about the rest, could give the impression of a Russian spy system so vast and powerful that it could only be fought effectively by the most extreme measures: liquidating all known communists, for example, and keeping all Russians abroad under personal supervision. That is to say, by doing the exact equivalent of what the Russians themselves do in their own country.

So it is a little reassuring, perhaps, to note some of the extraordinary blunders and weaknesses which the five cases in this book reveal. It is astonishing, for example, that Sorge's wireless operator should have been suppressing two-thirds of all his messages for nearly a year —and this at the most important period of his work— without being suspected either by Moscow or by Sorge himself. It is equally amazing that *Sisi*, writing from Switzerland to Germina Rabinowitch in Canada, should have had so little sense of secrecy that she put the full Moscow address of the Russian Military Intelligence in her letter. And it is no less odd that it should have taken Rabinowitch four and a half months to get in touch with Colonel Zabotin.

The Vavoudes Group, of course, broke every known rule of espionage, and it is only surprising that they survived so long—particularly as their masters were apparently quite prepared at any time to denounce half of them as police agents. Again, in Andersson's case some very strange mistakes were made. Why, for example, did the Russians (who must have known that their officials were liable to be watched) not use one or more contact-men between their spy and Anissimov and Orlov? And why was one of the bicycles used for passing instructions and reports clearly labelled (as it was) with Andersson's name, address and rank?

Of all five cases, however, the last revealed the biggest weaknesses. The communists claim northern Sweden as their stronghold. Yet Enbom had great difficulty in expanding his network, and in ten years could find no operator for his wireless. He and his companions completely ignored the rule that communist spies must immediately sever their open association with the Communist Party. And when Enbom broke with the Russians, they were apparently quite powerless to control him—and made no effort to do so—although it was nine months before he started to confess. (Here one should perhaps, in fairness, point out that he was the only one of the many spies mentioned in this book who did voluntarily break with the Russians, and the agony of his final breakdown is a striking illustration of the struggle all disillusioned communists have—not only the spies—in deserting their masters.)

Finally, most of the spies in all five cases broke the cardinal rule of espionage when they were arrested, which is—as Douglas Springhall knew—"admit nothing and refuse absolutely to talk."

It is not possible to make a satisfactory assessment of the real value to the Russians of the information which was stolen because, in some of the cases, the details of that information are still secret. Clearly, of course, the Russians thought it all extremely valuable, or they would not have made such efforts, and taken such risks, to get it. Sorge's reports were probably the most important to them, and Zabotin's Director in Moscow was highly pleased by some of the Colonel's work. Parts of the reports of Andersson and Enbom, too, seem to have been of considerable value.

In general, however, it is reasonable to guess that Russian espionage suffers from three big defects affecting the quality of its information, which should not apply to the intelligence services of other countries. The first arises from the fact that its spies are almost all fervent communists whose judgment is inevitably distorted by their rigid, stereotyped ways of thinking. Naturally, in military spying, this does not affect straightforward reports on, for example, the location of installations or the strength of units. But it may affect equally important reports on such matters as future intentions or morale. Communists, incidentally, have another general defect as spies (to be weighed against their many advantages) which is that they tend to become dominated by habits of thought, speech, behavior and even appearance which they may find it very difficult to control. This is a more important point than it may seem at first: several spies have actually betrayed themselves, and been caught, in this way. That is an added reason for the rule that the Russians' spies should dissociate themselves from their communist colleagues as soon as they begin spying.

The second defect is, perhaps, the most serious. The chief factor in successful espionage is the ability to evaluate information, and from it to build up a general picture. Occasionally, particularly during military operations, a single, specific item of information may be all-important—the immediate intentions of some enemy unit, for example, or the exact position of a ship. But usually—and especially in peacetime—it is the general picture which really counts. And this is precisely where the Russians must be weakest. The ability to evaluate correctly information from abroad must be very rare among their officials. Most of them have no experience of foreign countries, and even those who are sent abroad are so hemmed in by restrictions and precautions that (as the case of Gouzenko showed) they retain all kinds of extraordinary misconceptions. Besides, for a Soviet citizen to understand a "capitalist" country too well, might be to invite all kinds of personal dangers.

The atmosphere of mutual suspicion in which Russian officials inevitably live and work is the cause of the third big probable defect in their espionage system. It would be irrelevant to give details here of all the endless purges of Russian functionaries, high and low, which have gone on relentlessly since the time that Stalin began to consolidate his power, which Michael Padev computes as follows—*all the members of Lenin's first post-revolution Politbureau except Stalin, all the members of the new Politburo set up after Lenin's death except Stalin, five out of seven Presidents of the Central Executive Committee of the Soviets, 43 out of 54 Secretaries of the central party organization, three out of five Red Army Marshals, 70 out of 80 members of the Soviet War Council . . . it is an interminable list of* men liquidated as traitors, counter-revolutionaries or capitalist spies. In such conditions officials—in intelligence organizations above all—must be constantly aware of the personal danger they are in. With them the first consideration must always be to make the information they pass on fit what they think their superiors expect and want. And this must make the objective evaluation and presentation of information from espionage sources very difficult indeed.

For these and other reasons, it well may be that, in peacetime at least, the actual work done by Russian spy-rings is less harmful than it seems. It is even possible that the worst damage they do is the psychological damage caused by the knowledge that they exist. And, in this sense, even the failure of a spy-ring is a success. Certainly the story of Vladimir Petrov, of the Soviet Embassy at Canberra, the Canadian revelations, the Swedish cases and such other events as the arrest of Dr. Fuchs at the British atomic research establishment at Harwell, have had a powerfully unsettling effect. But one must also assume that in a war the use of communists as spies (and as saboteurs) would be on a far greater scale than in peacetime. No doubt the Russians are now quietly keeping many of their best spies and spy-rings in reserve. Andersson at least believed this, and was sorry that he had not been spared for "really big work" later on. To ignore the possible danger of that "really big work" would be unrealistic.

★　　　★　　　★

What then is the answer to the problem of the communists who spy for Russia? Their activities are only one part of the work of the illegal communist apparatus in each country. And that apparatus, in turn, is a part of each Communist Party. So the question of what can be done about the spies is linked to the much wider question of what a democracy should do to protect itself from all forms of communist attack—and that question is outside the scope of this book.

But at least there are three simple conclusions which seem clear.

First, the fewer communists there are in a country the fewer potential spies there will be for the Russians. As a general rule the number of communists is directly related to economic, social and political conditions. A prosperous, stable country has few communists; a country where there is poverty, injustice, and discontent is liable to have many more.

But even where communists are a tiny minority, they may still be a menace as saboteurs and spies—just as they may be a menace to political organizations or trade union branches. Therefore a democratic country or a democratic movement is wise to keep communists out of sensitive positions. But it will also be wise if it does this in such a way that the communists concerned are not able to pose as martyrs. For Communism, as the cases in this book clearly show, flourishes best in an atmosphere of secrecy and conspiracy and is most effective when it works underground. So to provide any unnecessary justification for that secrecy and conspiracy, or to force all communists underground, is to play straight into the hands of the men who run their spy-rings.

Finally, the more the facts are known about them, the harder it will be for Russian spy-masters and for men and women like those whose stories are told in this book to do their work.

Date Due

Printed in P.E.I. by Island Offset Inc.